George Grosz

GEORGE GROSZ

Frontispiece: Photograph of George Grosz, March 1954. Courtesy Ernest and Herta Pauli Ashton, Huntington, L. I., New York.

Library of Congress Catalogue Card Number 59-15105.
© 1960, Arts, Inc., 667 Madison Avenue, New York, N. Y.

Introduction by Ruth Berenson and Norbert Muhlen

and an Essay by the Artist · Edited by Herbert Bittner

A Golden Griffin book published by Arts, Inc., New York

Table of Contents

Publisher's Note

In this book we have attempted to present a general picture of the unique work of George Grosz rather than concentrate on one particular aspect of his multifacetted art. The book reveals the conflicting, igniting, torturous and dynamic elements in the work of this remarkable artist.

The introduction by Ruth Berenson and Norbert Muhlen, combining biography and evaluation, contributes to a better understanding of the man and his work.

The essay by the artist, written several years ago, was included at his own suggestion. It articulates admirably George Grosz' philosophy of life and art, as well as the nature of his inspiration.

This volume was initially planned by George Grosz himself and by his friend Herbert Bittner, our editor. It is a great misfortune that both passed away before it was completed. Their contribution to the preparation of this volume, however, has been invaluable. In long meetings before his departure for Germany in May, 1959, George Grosz worked with Herbert Bittner selecting, out of a collection of some 4,500 illustrations, sheets, and canvasses, most of the material included here. Grosz' desire was to present a sampling of all the major media which he had mastered, as well as to prove that — though in a different manner — his later work was as important as that of the German period.

We have tried to comply with this desire as much as possible. We can only hope that this volume which now is published as a memorial to the artist resembles as closely as possible what he would have liked it to be, and will contribute to the proper evaluation of his work.

The publishers wish to express their gratitude to all those who assisted in the preparation of this book, particularly to the following individuals and institutions who have made available original works and photographs for purposes of reproduction: Mr. and Mrs. Ernest B. Ashton, Huntington, Long Island, New York; Mrs. Maria Bittner, New York, New York; Mr. Erich Cohn, New York, New York; Mr. Walter Herlinger, New York, New York; Mr. Henry Regnery, Hinsdale, Illinois; Mr. Bernard Reis, New York, New York; Mrs. Kate T. Steinitz, Los Angeles, California; Mr. Adolph Tausik, New York, New York; Mr. Arnott J. White, New York, New York; Dr. William N. Young, Halesite,

Long Island, New York; The Baltimore Museum of Art, Baltimore, Maryland; Fogg Art Museum, Harvard University, Cambridge, Massachusetts; Galleries of Cranbrook Academy of Art, Bloomfield Hills, Michigan; The Metropolitan Museum of Art, New York, New York; The Museum of Modern Art, New York, New York; Rochester Memorial Art Gallery, Rochester, New York; Whitney Museum of American Art, New York, New York; The Wichita Art Museum, Wichita, Kansas; *Life* Magazine.

For their special assistance, we should like to thank Miss Dorothy Irvine of the Whitney Museum of American Art, Miss Agnes Mongan of the Fogg Art Museum, and Mr. Peter Selz of The Museum of Modern Art as well as the entire staff of The Museum of Modern Art Library.

We are also deeply grateful to Mrs. Maria Bittner for her wholehearted cooperation, to Mr. Erich Cohn for valuable information, to Mr. Arnott J. White, the artist's devoted disciple, for his generous contribution in time and advice in the many instances in which we have consulted him, to Mr. Lewis Birdseye for his assistance in the preparation of the bibliography and to Miss Zita Vlavianos for her manifold editorial assistance.

Thanks are due as well to Mr. James Barnett, Mr. Sanford M. Herman, Mr. Frank Petrocelli, Mr. Alfred L. Schaeffer, Mr. Ladislav Sutnar for their expert advice.

THE PUBLISHERS

New York, New York, July 1960

The Two Worlds of George Grosz

Writers on art tend to prefer artists who can be easily pigeonholed — who travel armed, as it were, with a passport clearly listing their characteristics: their dates, their school, their place of residence in the art world, plus any special marks of identification. George Grosz, however, defies such easy classification. His work cannot be given an easy descriptive brand name or fitted into any of the artistic "isms" of the twentieth century.

Born in Berlin on July 26, 1893, where he died on July 6, 1959 after having spent his last 27 years in the United States, critics are not agreed on whether Grosz was an American or German artist. They have been unable to decide whether he was primarily a draughtsman or a painter, a social satirist or a surrealist bewitched by symbols, a cartoonist or a visionary — or whether he was not, perhaps, a unique mixture of all these. Some writers think of him as a period piece of Germany's Weimar Republic which, in his Berlin youth, he graphically depicted and "unmasked." Many have filed him away as this and nothing more, glossing over the work of his years in America as if, by the mere fact of his migration, his artistic power had been suddenly amputated. Having safely and satisfactorily labeled the German George Grosz, it has been easier for them to ignore the American George Grosz, whose achievements were so very different. Fascinated by the youthful revolutionary artist, who was certainly exciting enough, many were reluctant to take up the problem presented by the older man whose work bore little relation to that which they knew so well.

What is certain is that the transatlantic transplantation of Grosz at the age of 39 brought about a complete change of his art in style and subject, form and substance, technique and intent. This alone sets him apart from those other major European painters — Max Beckmann, Marc Chagall, Max Ernst, Salvador Dali, Raoul Dufy, Fernand Léger — who came to America as refugees during the war years. On none of these did America exercise an appreciable effect; their art remained substantially what it had been in Europe and when, with the exception of Beckmann, they returned to Europe after 1945, they resumed their careers as if nothing had happened. Unlike them Grosz came to America in 1932 of his own free will. He was not a refugee to whom America meant little more than a temporary haven, but an immigrant who intended to become fully American — an American citizen and an American artist. The process of Americanization occupied him for the rest of his life.

A little aggressively, as if he wanted to decry a contradiction which no one except, perhaps, his inner self had voiced, he used to proclaim to his friends, "I am an American!" When in the summer of 1953 he revisited his native Berlin for the first time in twenty years, he carefully outfitted himself with loud neckties, pastel-colored silk suits and a rakish Panama hat — he looked exactly like a European caricature of "a typical Yankee." At a solemn reunion with old schoolmates, now all dignified middle-aged burghers, he proudly explained that his American suit was so expensive because it was moth-proof, rain-proof, and, he added with dead-pan seriousness, "suicide-proof, too." A few years later while taking a walk with him near his house on Long Island, we reminded him of this scene which he had forgotten. After thinking about it a minute he said, "And soon they will invent an even more expensive suit in which everyone can kill himself in his own fashion."

But when visitors waxed enthusiastic or nostalgic about Europe, as happened often, and when he had one glass too many, as happened even more often, he would interrupt them, stretching his long legs out in front of him, and would point to the soles of his shoes in fascination, saying, "Here are my little American roots — can't you see my little roots?" When people asked him how long he had lived in America, he would answer, "Since I died in Germany."

Although born in Berlin, Grosz, the offspring of North German peasants and craftsmen, spent his childhood in Pomerania, one of Germany's most provincial backwaters, where, in the small town of Stolp, his widowed mother supported her family by running the officers' mess of a fashionable Prussian regiment. At thirteen Grosz, already something of a rebel, was expelled from high school for hitting a teacher. On the advice of his old drawing master, but against his mother's wishes for she feared he would be unable to earn his living, he decided to study art. He spent two years at the Academy in Dresden and in 1911 enrolled at the Academy in Berlin where he was awarded a scholarship. Like most talented students of his generation, he was bored by academic studies, and soon started cutting his classes. These were so stultified that he was not even permitted to work in oils but forced to confine himself to drawing from the antique. The work of *avant-gardistes* such as Munch, Hodler and Pascin, a friend of his Berlin teacher, was far more exciting to him. In addition, he became fascinated by the German version of *Art Nouveau* — *Jugendstil* — which he studied in the popular comic weeklies. He soon discovered his own gift for caricature, and even before he left Dresden, when he was only sixteen, he sold his first cartoon to *Ulk,* a supplement of the famous Berlin paper, the *Berliner Tageblatt.* Before long, with such gently humorous vignettes as *Clowns and Dogs* (1915) drawn in the curvilinear patterns of *Jugendstil* which were even then somewhat outdated, he was making enough money to support himself.

By 1913 he had saved enough for a trip to Paris which, however, had little effect on his art. More important to him than Picasso and Matisse were the cartoons of Wilhelm Busch, the grandfather of the modern comic-strip (his *Max and Moritz* inspired the earliest American comic strip, the *Katzenjammer Kids*) whom he revered all his life as "one of the few German humorists." The first important foreign influence on Grosz came not from France but from Italy, in the form of the romantic dynamism of the Futurists who were exhibited in Berlin toward the end of 1913. He was just beginning to incorporate their semi-cubist distortions into his own curvilinear drawings of Berlin cafés and street scenes when the war broke out.

Grosz' enlistment in the infantry marked the first decisive turning point in his life. Before the war he had been, he remembered, "a friendlier person than I am now," but his first-hand experience with what seemed to him the farce of military discipline and with the death and destruction of the trenches filled him with rage, hate, and a determination to hit back at "the ruling order." Twice hospitalized among severely wounded and mentally disturbed soldiers, he barely saved his own sanity by pouring out his disillusionment into the vitriolic drawings by which he first became famous.

On his return to Berlin in 1918, he joined the juvenile rebellion of Dada — "not that," as he explained later, "any of us knew what Dadaism actually was." As "Propagandada" he paraded through the avenues of Berlin wearing a Death's Head and carrying a poster emblazoned, *"Dada, Dada ueber alles!"* He also did illustrations for Dada publications with titles like *Jedermann sein eigner Fussball (Everybody his own football); Die Pleite (Stone Broke);* and *Der blutige Ernst (Dead Serious).* In these and other drawings of 1917-1922 the influence of Italian Futurism can be seen in the doubled outlines and rays which crisscross the picture surface, giving an impression of movement and chaos. The influence of Cubism is evident, too, and more importantly, that of Paul Klee who anticipated the Dadaists in his interest in the art of children and the insane;

13

Grosz, too, tried to recapture their naiveté. He also studied the cinema technique of photomontage as can be seen in his use of superposed planes.

Around 1922 he began to shed these mannerisms and to render the life about him with greater realism. This, perhaps, was a result of his trip to the Soviet Union that same year. Like so many German intellectuals of the period, especially those associated with Dada, Grosz' violent hatred of war and the "ruling order" had led him to sympathize with Communism. But what he saw in Moscow and Leningrad filled him with a lasting disgust, an almost physical repulsion for Leftism, whether in art, politics or everyday life. The ubiquitous poverty and filth were as depressing as the interminable wrangling of Communist intellectuals on the merits of Constructivism and Socialist Realism. The former was then still permissible though to Grosz, who was never attracted by abstraction, it seemed ludicrously antiseptic. The latter, with its doctrinaire emphasis on uplifting the masses, seemed equally false and also archaistic. On his return to Berlin he determined to steer clear of partisan movements and schools in order to develop his own personal style. He would no longer try to translate his views into symbols derived from others. Instead, his pockets full of pencils and notebooks, he would paint and sketch what he saw with his own eyes.

If he had abandoned Marxism, he had lost none of his loathing of the existing system which had prompted it; and he seemed to have an inner need to pour salt on the open wound of his disgust by seeking out just those places — the luxurious restaurants, the theatres, the flop houses, the slums — which showed it at its worst. Grosz' Berlin is populated exclusively by beggars, black marketeers, whores, pimps, cripples, generals, drunks, panderers, the gluttons and the starving, seducers and seduced, all killing, drinking, lusting, fornicating in perennial nausea. They have nothing in common with each other but their depravity. Like Daumier, he drew a *Comédie Humaine,* but unlike the Frenchman, who pitied his victims even while he mocked them, and whose comedy therefore was occasionally tinged with sadness, Grosz had no compassion. His Seven Deadly Sins were not balanced by any redeeming Virtues; as he wrote later, "I made careful drawings but I had no love of the people, either inside or out. I was arrogant enough to consider myself as a natural scientist, not as a painter or satirist. I thought about right and wrong but my conclusions were always unfavorable to all men equally."

These drawings displayed a mastery of line and a respect for details which marked Grosz not only an heir of Daumier but of the great German draughtsmen of the Renaissance — Dürer, Holbein and Grünewald. In his desire to "un-

14

mask" the appearances, and to depict what seemed to him the inner reality, he often had recourse to a rather literal device: he outlined the nude bodies — mostly of women, and particularly their sexual characteristics — in addition to their clothing. As time passed, his wish to be as objective as a "natural scientist" led him around 1926 to approach the *Neue Sachlichkeit,* a movement which advocated the artist's complete emotional disengagement from his subject. Grosz greatly admired its foremost exponent, Otto Dix, who executed painstakingly realistic portraits in the manner of a Van Eyck or Memling. In a similar vein Grosz painted a number of sober detailed portraits of his mother-in-law, Anna Peter, the writer Max Hermann-Neisse, and other friends. Though he never officially joined the group, perhaps as much because of his decision to avoid "isms" of all kinds as because he was constitutionally unable to divorce his inner self from his work, the *Neue Sachlichkeit* exercised an important influence on his art, cleansing it of the last lingering clichés of modernism. He never reverted to the wilful chaos of Dada, nor was he ever again tempted by the symbols of abstraction, let alone abstract expressionism.

In the decade before 1932 Grosz must have drawn and painted (mostly in watercolor) literally thousands of square-necked bourgeois, drunkards, derelicts, monocled officers, fat wives and leering prostitutes, that cast of characters of the *Berlin Café,* and also of the *Dreigroschen Oper* by Bert Brecht and Kurt Weill. These images, in fact, came to personify, in many German and foreign eyes, the Germany of the Weimar Republic, while Grosz himself became both famous and notorious, the *enfant terrible* of the time. The titles of his books and portfolios reflect the mocking bitterness which earned him his reputation: *Das Gesicht der Herrschenden Klasse (The Face of the Ruling Class),* 1919; *Gott mit Uns (God with Us),* 1920; *Ecce Homo* 1922; *Spiesserspiegel (Mirror of Boobs)* 1924; *Ueber alles die Liebe (Love Above All)* 1931.

Grosz' deliberately ironic use of titles such as *Ecce Homo* and *Spiesserspiegel,* both of which recalled to Germans the accomplishments of the great German woodcutters and engravers of the Renaissance, infuriated the "ruling class," or more precisely, the district attorney, who attempted rather ineffectually to fight back. In 1920 the artist was tried for libelling the army and fined 5,000 marks. In 1923 the publication of *Ecce Homo* led to his conviction for blasphemy (he had shown a prostitute wearing a cross) and also for "corrupting the sense of shame and virtue innate to the German people." This time he was fined 6,000 marks (only a few pennies in inflated currency) and twenty-four plates of the portfolio were confiscated. In 1928 he was again tried for blasphemy, this time for a draw-

15

ing of the crucified Christ in a gas mask, an illustration to Jaroslav Hašek's *Good Soldier Schweik*. The uproar over this seems surprising today; the drawing reflects rather the anger of a modern Savonarola at the corruption of the multitude than irreverence, and the conviction was reversed the following year. Grosz thoroughly enjoyed these occasions, which naturally served to increase his fame — and his sales.

Grosz, indeed, made a lot of money during the 1920's. Those members of the ruling class whom he so bitterly satirized and whose position he subverted, vied among each other to buy his pictures, just as they enthusiastically packed theatres presenting the equally destructive plays which Brecht wrote, and Erwin Piscator staged in the spirit of the "class struggle." The bourgeoisie was not scared by revolutionary slogans; on the contrary, they were amused, entertained and grateful. Equally grateful were the parlor pinks who were the real "ruling class" of Berlin's cultural life in the '20's. They saw to it that Grosz achieved international renown for transforming their slogans into unforgettable graphic form.

But unlike them, Grosz was not a true revolutionary; he was more of a revolutionary poseur. He thought of himself as an "individualist" and regarded the masses with contempt if not hatred. For those who claimed to speak in their name his disdain was equally bitter. "Among the masses", he said, "I found scorn, mockery, fear, oppression, falsehood, betrayal, lies and filth ... I have never indulged in worshipping them, even when I pretended to believe in certain political theories ..."

For more than ten years Grosz was preoccupied with rendering in acid "the naked truth" about the world he hated. What resulted was "a Walpurgisnacht" (as Paul Valéry described the nineteenth century French magazine *La Caricature* in which Daumier appeared), "a Satanic comedy riotous to the point of debauchery, now pure tomfoolery, now avid with the lust for blood."

In 1932, to his great surprise, Grosz was invited to teach at the Art Students League in New York. He accepted immediately.

Although it was only a year before the Hitler nightmare, few of Grosz' Berlin friends took the Nazi menace seriously; rather, they expected that before long there would be a Communist revolution in Germany. To this left-wing circle, America was not a promised land but a capitalist hell. But Grosz did not agree with them. "From my first birthday," he told us, "I was homesick for America," and recalled that with the very first money he had earned when he sold his car-

16

toon to *Ulk* as a sixteen-year old, he had bought a pair of "American shoes, — guaranteed genuine," to whose soles, perhaps, clung those seeds of fantasy from which, years later, his "little American roots" would germinate. He was still in his teens when he Americanized his name from Georg to George.

In the first essay ever written about the young Grosz — as early as 1916 — his literary discoverer, the German expressionist poet Theodor Däubler, stressed his "cowboy romanticism, his yearning for skyscrapers . . ." Even "in his drawing of a nude," Däubler observed, "Grosz expresses his wistful longing for New York . . . reflected in the heart of Berlin . . ." With remarkable insight, Däubler added that "essentially his view of the big city is apocalyptic; he sees its cosmic, perhaps meteoric image in which hearses emerge, . . . express trains speed over each other like a thunderstorm, . . . and the houses are geometric, naked as if briefly after a bombardment . . ." In 1917 when Grosz was in the army and his disgust and bitterness had brought him to the edge of despair, he painted a charming watercolor of a skyscraper city which he titled in English, *I Remember New York*, and during the early twenties he used to entertain his Dada friends with mysterious tales of his American ancestors — a reflection, of course, of a profound wish-dream.

His image of America was formed during his childhood from the reading of the *Leatherstocking Tales, The Last of the Mohicans*, and, even more, the adventure stories of Karl May which, still today, are a staple of German schoolboys. From these writers emerged the picture of a Rousseau-like land, peopled by Indians and soldiers of fortune, wild and tempting with its limitless prairies, its limitless opportunities, its faith in the resources of freedom and the future. This was the America toward which he was drawn. He was also seeking, quite literally, the fruits of that much-maligned Wall Street capitalism, the pot of gold at the end of the rainbow.

His fame as a wild revolutionary had preceded him, and on his arrival in the spring of 1932, a number of reporters were on hand to receive him. But they were rather disappointed. "Mild Monster Arrives," snorted *Time Magazine*, commenting regretfully on the contrast between what they had expected and the gentle and friendly man who greeted them. Nevertheless, his reputation as a monster served him well, securing him from the beginning both pupils and public attention.

The New York which Grosz saw seemed to him the embodiment of his youthful dreams. The skyscrapers glistened in the morning sun; gangsters and cowboys slept in the open wilds of Central Park; tough guys hunched over their beers in

Columbus Avenue saloons, and the Broadway lights turned night into day. It was exactly as he had imagined it — and painted it — before. But there was a different reality behind this dream world which he did not see. The skyscrapers were empty; the sleepers in the park were respectable unemployed who had nowhere to go; the lights of Broadway shone down on breadlines and apple vendors, and many of the drinkers were spending their last dime to forget their hunger and hopelessness.

It was, of course, the worst year of the depression. All America was in ferment, especially the artists and intellectuals; as the floors of their houses caved in, the ceilings above them collapsed. The floor was America's economic and social order which, until then, had provided most of them with a modicum of material security; the ceiling was the culture of Europe to which, for more than a century, they had looked up in search of inspiration and which suddenly now seemed as empty and ugly as their own. In their material and spiritual panic they loathed and rejected the face of their own "ruling class" whose order had proved so wanting. It was the onset of America's "Red Decade" of the thirties — and the New York in which Grosz found himself in fact differed little from the Berlin he had so gladly abandoned. True, no Hitler loomed on the American horizon, but the atmosphere of despair and rebellion seemed similar, with the same radical slogans in the air. It was little wonder that the famous Berlin revolutionary, the satirist of "the ruling class", the "artist of the class struggle" was greeted by his New York colleagues with great expectations.

But Grosz never understood this. The New York he saw and painted during his first American years had nothing to do with the depression, and the contrast between the well-fed and the starving, the slums and the luxury apartment houses which preoccupied most American writers and artists during the thirties (and turned so many of them into Communists) — in brief, his own old Berlin theme — almost did not exist for him. While he roamed the city with his sketchbooks, he hardly noticed the breadlines and the beggars; all he saw was the land of Karl May and Fennimore Cooper with its limitless possibilities, where everything was tinged with gold. Once, while still in Berlin, a reporter had asked Grosz where he thought paradise was located, and he had replied, "In the Rocky Mountains." Nothing he saw ever caused him to change his mind. Years later, when the museum of Dallas gave him a one man show, he took off for Texas feeling like a pioneer, and returned beaming with boyish pride at the ten-gallon hat and cowboy boots he had been given, refusing to take them off, even at dinner. Reality never impinged on his dream.

18

Grosz might have looked at America more critically had he not fared so well from the very beginning. His paintings and drawings sold, his classes were popular, and he was given numerous commissions for magazine and book illustrations. He never wondered why he was so successful at a time when most American artists would have starved had it not been for the WPA. He would never have understood that rich Americans bought his Berlin pictures for the same reasons the rich Berliners had — because they took a kind of masochistic pleasure in seeing themselves and their capitalist world unmasked, and because to buy such pictures helped assuage their feelings of guilt for still having enough money to buy anything. Grosz could not see this — for such an insight would have destroyed his image of America. Similarly, he ignored American painters of protest like Philip Evergood, Ben Shahn and Jack Levine who had been greatly influenced by Grosz' art and considered themselves his disciples. Moreover, he felt unable to fulfill the expectations of those who wanted him to debunk America as he had Germany. "Scratch their eyes out, George," said Alexander King, then editor of a short-lived magazine, *Americana,* which had commissioned some drawings. But Grosz did not scratch out any eyes, he did not even deliver his drawings. "For me, something of that spirit had died," he wrote later.

Grosz' Americanization did not follow the familiar pattern in which the cells of the immigrant's European soul gradually wither away to be replaced by New World ones eventually to produce an altogether new, American Adam. Grosz deliberately left his European self behind him when he stepped off the gangplank; he was, as it were, completely nude, armed only with brushes and palette, ready to equip himself on arrival with a brand-new, ready-made American self. His was a conscious choice of which he was completely aware; sometimes he would act it out to his friends — *"der alte Georg,"* the mixture of a Prussian recruit and a hate-ridden street brawler, would turn into "George, the man from Manhattan," a cross between a businessman and a clown.

The reasons for his complete rejection of his human and artistic past are not altogether clear. Had he succumbed to that "American optimism" which was such an integral part of his boyhood image of America? Did he believe that by not dipping his brush in acid, he would more easily become Americanized? Or had the turbulent Berlin years exhausted his raging aggression, so that he had to find a new content, as well as a new form, for his art as aging angry young men often do? Had he come to see satire as a one-dimensional, and hence a sterile minor art form? Perhaps all these factors were operative. At any rate, from the moment of his arrival, he tried to make a *tabula rasa* of his German past.

But as easy as it had been for him as a twenty-year old in Berlin to find his own style and stick to it for more than a decade, so it was difficult for him now, a man of forty, to evolve a new personal means of expression. For the rest of his life he was to go on searching.

His first ambition, as he often said, was to be a second Norman Rockwell. In 1960, Rockwell himself described the purpose of his art as an illustrator: "The view of life I communicate in my pictures excludes the sordid and the ugly. I paint life as I would like it to be."[1] Naturally such a purpose was diametrically opposed to what Grosz had done in Berlin — which was doubtless why it appealed to him now. In his illustrations for *Hansel and Gretel* and *Snow White*, Grosz was trying to do just that. But though he worked hard he did not succeed. Years later he showed us some of the sketchbooks containing vignettes of New York — from the nursemaids in Central Park to the stripteasers of 42nd Street — in which he had tried to work *a la manière de Rockwell*. But in each there was a graphic irony, a backwash of sensuous sadness which set them apart from popular illustrations.

Apart from teaching and executing the illustrations which had been commissioned, Grosz devoted his first years in this country to serious study. Beside the German Renaissance masters who had appealed to him, he knew little of the art of the past; now he began to frequent the Metropolitan Museum and the Frick Collection, studying Rubens and Boucher, Fragonard and Magnasco, whose swirling, thick impasto particularly appealed to him. He sketched a great deal, first in New York and later, after the arrival of his wife and sons, in Long Island near his house in Douglaston.

During the first couple of years, he painted mainly in watercolor, as he had in Berlin. His first attempts yielded mainly colored drawings but gradually he evolved a new technique adaptable to the demands of rendering light and atmosphere, which previously had not interested him. Around 1936 he started to work in oil, which he had not studied seriously before. He became fascinated by its unlimited technical possibilities — the different effects which could be obtained by underpainting, glazing, scumbling, thick and thin impastos, with palette knives, with brushes of varying sizes and textures. Often he painstakingly noted his methods on the backs of his canvases. In later years he not only made his own brushes of carefully graduated shapes and sizes, but also often ground his own pigments, experimentally varying their texture by mixing them with sand and wax, and even with Coca Cola.

During these years, it was as if Grosz were attending school for the second time, but now there were no social or political diversions; he concentrated solely on mastering his own craft. To those critics who wondered, as did the writer for *Art Digest,* "Is Grosz slipping?" or, as did Milton Brown who titled his review in *Parnassus,* "Death of an Artist," Grosz was defiant. "It was not an escape, it was a new beginning," he said, repeatedly emphasizing this in his splendidly written autobiographical essays, *A Little Yes and a Big No,* which he published in 1946.

In 1939 Grosz and his family spent a year at Wellfleet, on Cape Cod, and it was here that he promoted himself to the next class of his autodidactic school. Nature and the female nude became his subjects — dunes, blades of grass, insects, the fold of drapery of his wife's clothing casually thrown over a chair, and the nude herself, as glorious, as boldly sensual as those of Rubens and Fragonard. It seemed to him that his "Americanization" was somehow reflected in the way he was able to see and reproduce these peaceful aspects of an idyllic world — but now his Americanization no longer meant, as it had previously, an abrupt break with his personal past, but rather a reevaluation of the whole European artistic past, from Dürer and Holbein to Rubens and Renoir, from the mysticism of Grünewald to that of Munch and Ensor.

For much as he tried, Grosz could not resist seeking the inner reality behind appearances. "There is more to a rainfall than merely rain," he once remarked. In the landscape of Cape Cod he saw more than the dunes thinly covered with dried grass and twisted pines; his studies of nature and the nude, at first so simple and almost naively pretty, grew threatening and weird. The sensuous woman — a bather or a nymph, her curves outlined in red in the manner of Fragonard, a symbol of voluptuous joy — serves only as a contrast to the dessicated earth. Often the dunes have anthropomorphic shapes which recall stretched-out human figures — murdered, violated, or perhaps in concupiscent expectation, under a phosphorescent reflection of fire and brimstone. Did Grosz, out of all the fertile teaming landscapes America offered, deliberately choose to paint one of its most barren — the bare dunes of Cape Cod and Long Island, because their very emptiness coincided with a new need, a vague premonition of coming disaster? His eyes transformed the Cape countryside, which to most evoked the image of peaceful summer days at the seashore, into a world in crisis, sinful and cowering under the lightning which signaled approaching catastrophe. The inner realities which he now saw behind the visible appearances were of a kind very different from the somewhat juvenile sexuality he had outlined and "unmasked" behind the clothing of his Berlin figures. "Next to me there is always a hell," he once said — and perhaps this was why he called one of these almost apocalyptic landscapes, endless dunes mirroring the lurid flames of a sunset, *End of the World*.

Without meaning to, once again Grosz was obeying Daumier's dictum: *"Il faut être de son temps."* But now his vision would no longer confine itself to the particular but would embrace the timeless. He had travelled in the hate-distorted realm of ugliness and in the equally twisted land of all-too-pure prettiness, and he knew his way around both. Now he would venture into uncharted territory, there to attempt to convey his own awesome vision of our time.

In Huntington, Long Island, where he lived after 1946 — that is, where he painted, drank and wrestled with his demons — Grosz was known as an eccentric local character whose peculiarities were accepted due to his position in the world. He continued teaching at the Art Students League, and also held private classes for some of his Long Island neighbors. His pictures, both old and new, continued to sell. As the years passed, he gradually acquired a new mask — that of a successful business man who loved to shock his listener by claiming that all he cared about was making money and that an artist who was poor was no artist. At the same time, his alcoholic addiction grew. He explained to Dr. Richard Huelsenbeck, his old friend, former fellow-Dadaist, physician and psychoanalyst: "That's the only way I can endure life."

When he was on the wagon, he often was gloomy and silent, but at other times he entertained the company with his monologues on a single theme — a verse, perhaps, or just a single word that had caught his fancy. "I talk the way Paul Klee paints," he once said to us — but he also talked the way he himself painted, obsessively concentrating on a single subject, its different aspects and potentials.

When conversation came around to politics, he fell silent. But he was sick at what was going on in Germany. During his first years in this country he painted a few factual representations of the Nazi horror, such as *After the Questioning* (1935). But such anecdotes, rather reminiscent of his Berlin pictures, failed to satisfy the sense of dread and foreboding which, as early as 1934, had prompted *The Punishment*, a water color showing the flaming ruins of a bombed metropolis — two years before the first actual bombing of an open city inspired Picasso's *Guernica*.

A feeling of impending doom haunted Grosz with increasing persistence during the late thirties and early forties as one can see from the drawings of *Interregnum*, published in 1936. In the following years, even while he continued to

22

paint occasional nudes, landscapes and still lifes, he embarked on a series of pictures in which he attempted to express his apocalyptic vision of a world bent on self-destruction, of an Armageddon whose only survivors would be a race of skeletons or scarecrow-like "Stickmen".

The spirit which permeates these pictures is utterly different from that of the Berlin cartoons and caricatures. Then, like Daumier, he had bitterly satirized human foibles and pretenses, depicting, in the words of Hans Sedlmayr, "a secularized hell under the banner of the comic."[2] Now, like Goya he tried to show that man's self-destructiveness is the totality of evil. The ruins are not those of specific places but the mirror of crumbling civilization; his dictator is not Napoleon, nor Hitler, nor Stalin (though often he resembles all three) but the embodiment of brute force in power; his victim is no longer a Jew, an anti-Nazi, an anti-Communist, but Everyman, caught in the struggle between misery and greatness, between the instincts of the animal and the image of the Creator, between the end of the world and the emergence of "the new earth."

Grosz had learned much from Goya. But even more important were his own memories of Germany's Gothic past, of Grimm's fairy tales, of the heritage which produced Goethe's *Walpurgisnacht* and the fantasies of Grünewald and Bosch. Grosz readily admitted this, and doubtless agreed with the statement of John I. H. Baur, his most emphatic critic, who said, "Paradoxically the artist became, in some ways, more Teutonic here than he had been in Germany."

It is perhaps strange that at a time when, externally, at least, the mask of "George, the Man from Manhattan" had replaced that of *"Der alte Georg"*, he should have become aware of the strength of these sources. But as he somewhat ruefully confessed in *A Little Yes and a Big No,* he was beginning to learn that there were limits beyond which his Americanization could not go. "Although I tried to imitate Walt Whitman," he wrote ". . . and even succeeded in gaining the reputation of being a positive, happy, smiling contented optimist — there still remained in me something unchangeable, something I consider schizophrenic — a margin of inflexibility that was like a mighty immovable stone."

Did this reference to schizophrenia point to the strange split personality which went on painting idyllic nudes and landscapes simultaneously with visions as terrifying as those of Bosch? Or was he thinking of the disparity between his dark Teutonic past and those "little American roots" he had tried so hard to nurture? What is certain is that schizophrenia did not affect the exercise of his craft. He had become a consummate master not only in the expressiveness of his draughtsmanship but in the use of oil which he handled like a virtuoso. With cold objectivity and minute accuracy he rendered the horrors which haunted him trying, as he said, "to recreate my world as realistically as possible . . . because the more of a nightmare it is, the more I must recreate it in an understanding way." Even before the actual outbreak of World War II Grosz was haunted by premonitions, and the signing of the Armistice did little to assuage his feeling of despair and dread of the future. The main body of his work from 1936 to 1949 is concerned with the single subject of man's self-destructiveness and his struggle for life. He treated the theme by devising sub-themes whose ramifications he explored with inexhaustible energy. Thus, there are a series of paintings of skeletons whose cavorting antics recall Holbein's *Totentanz*; a series deals with the plight of the lone human survivor in a wilderness of slime and destruction (as in *The Wanderer*) or in the world of a new master race (*The Ambassador of Good Will*); a series of what Baur has called "ruins," such as *A Piece of My World I,* in which, as early as 1938, Grosz seemed to foretell the devastation of a Hiroshima. Sometimes, as in *The Pit* (1946) he used an abundance of Surrealist symbols, medieval allegories and modern anecdotal imagery to heighten the impact of his nightmare. This picture, which Baur considers Grosz' greatest, owes more to the art of Bosch and Grünewald, which it resembles not only in theme but in composition and refulgent color, than to anything produced in the twentieth century. But unlike its Gothic precursors, *The Pit* offers little hope of redemption.

Indeed, Grosz' pessimism increased as he continued to search for an image which would give expression to his visions. The Stickmen series, which occupied him from 1947 to 1949, seems to be his final answer. Their ancestors, in Grosz' cosmogony, are to be found in the lone survivors: as early as 1943 the ragged figures confronting the *Ambassador of Good Will,* with their emaciated and enlarged heads, foreshadow the Stickmen. But it was only in 1947 that Grosz hit upon their final ghostly shape; they appear as the clowns of the Apocalypse.

Hardly had he invented them, with their giant heads, bulbous insect-like eyes, hairy skeletons and limbs of joined sticks recalling spiders — when they took on a life of their own, almost independent of their creator who sat back and observed their Dance of Death, or, more precisely, their Rock 'n' Roll of Death; for in all their timelessness, they are very much a part of our time. In their grey world of mud, barbed wire and ruins (most of the series is in monochromatic watercolors) these empty-headed fanatics, at once both comic and tragic as fanatics often are, desperately try, through their sheer manic activity, to save — what? We are never told; are they, perhaps, like the faceless tramps of Samuel Beckett whom they so closely resemble, waiting for Godot?

24

The concern with the theme of annihilation and destruction, which has preoccupied so many painters and sculptors of the 1950's, shows Grosz once more to have been ahead of his time. His elongated Stickmen prophesy the gaunt figures of Giacometti, and like them, inhabit an infinite barrenness symbolizing not only the abdication of the intellect but of the creative spirit; while his almost obsessive use of the hole — in the torn banner which a Stickman is raising, in the torn canvas which a Stickman paints, in the torn music which a Stickman plays, — seems related to the sculpture of Henry Moore where the void is substituted for the solid, an empty cavity for the fertility of the womb. But in a literal interpretation, one discerns bravery and faith in the stubborness with which the Stickmen, these ruins of men in a ruined world, keep pursuing their ruined art; there remains human dignity in this apocalyptic clown, who in his fashion still seeks beauty and truth.

Possessed of an inborn vitality which did not easily permit him to surrender to the ubiquity of nothingness, Grosz continued searching for a saving grace, or at least a meaning. He had not lost his belief that man must continue to resist evil. Once, when a critic asked whether he saw any hope for our time, he answered: "Perhaps the female is our hope . . . When I paint the Woman she stands solid and unafraid, sensual and warm above the Chaos." There are no Women in the Stickmen's world, but in all the apparently senseless activity one is left wondering if, after all, there is not some purpose. Grosz hoped so: in *Waving the Flag*, the Stickman proudly brandishes aloft the rainbow banner which, he noted, "stands for the symbols man once believed in — symbols which are forbidden in this grey world of mine."

In all his painting — and thinking — of this period, the two dominating symbols remained the grey color, standing for the enemy and end of man, and the rainbow colors signalling survival and hope. The rainbow, though torn and tattered, never disappeared from his imagery.

After 1949, Grosz' prolific creative powers seemed to fail him. The few nudes and landscapes which he painted in the 1950's are little more than self-plagiarism. There was an occasional flash of his old inspiration. In 1953 *Life* magazine commissioned him to illustrate the escape story of a Pole, Marek Korowicz, who had defected to the West while a member of the Polish U.N. delegation. Grosz saw in Korowicz' description of Communist Poland a confirmation of his earlier grim forebodings. In his *Life* drawings, the dictator, no longer a composite of Napoleon, Hitler and Stalin, is now a beast in Russian uniform, his mouth a gaping maw through which one sees the naked sky. The victim is a descendant of Stickman — but his eyes are sewn shut, his ears are plugged up, and in place of his heart there is a hole, laced with barbed wire against which can be seen the outline of a man's head and a clenched fist. In one corner, drunken soldiers shoot crap; in the opposite corner, a pious crowd of pilgrims, realistically drawn, enter the open doors of the Cathedral of St. Mary of Katowice, a famous Polish shrine. There is a marked contrast between this vividly rendered grey world of totalitarianism, whose meaning and message he depicted in final, unequalled, exhaustive depth, and the more conventional sketches of the rainbow world of New York and Paris, to which Korowicz escaped; they were probably taken from some of his old notebooks.

In 1954, when he had largely ceased to create, Grosz finished one new painting, a strange face of a clown in almost child-like, poster-brilliant water colors which seems unrelated to any other work of his past. He gave it the enigmatic title, *Hommage à Gogol* — in memory of the Russian writer who, like Grosz, had started as a social satirist, written his main work in exile, but burned what he considered best in it — the mystical, religious second part of the *Dead Souls* — after his return to his native land nine days before his death. Did Grosz perceive his own fate in Gogol's?

Probably the last painting Grosz ever did is the brilliant water color, *Old Man Watering Flowers*. All his old technical mastery is there — but the figure resembles nothing he had done before. It has no weight, no bones — it is only a shadow. Was this, perhaps, a last self-portrait? Is Grosz saying with Candide, *"Après tout, il faut cultiver notre jardin?"*

The thought of returning to Germany scared Grosz. When in 1950 a delegate to the Congress of Cultural Freedom called him on the telephone from West Berlin to ask him to come, he wept for five minutes without being able to stop; then he cried, *"Ich kann nicht!"*, and hung up.

Finally in 1953 he was persuaded to go for a visit. With a brand new wardrobe he masked himself as the funny "Man from Manhattan," flew to Berlin, received some commissions for stage sets and book illustrations, waited for great honors which did not come, painted a few run-of-the-mill sketches on a two-week trip to Bavaria, and returned to Huntington where he entertained his friends with the typical reports of a Yankee tourist — how he was cheated changing dollars to marks, how awful the whisky and the plumbing were, and how shocked he had been by the sinful night life of Berlin and Munich.

He wanted no truck with his past, not even to be reminded of it. When a Berlin reporter asked him whether the city was still as comic as it had been before, he threatened him: "Unless you scram, I'll throw you out!" Later he explained to us: "I won't let him sick the ghosts of my past on me!" Another Berlin newsman asked whether he liked America or Germany best. "Look," said Grosz, fishing his house key from his pocket, "in Europe you have to have a key to get into your house, and without it they will leave you to die. At home in Huntington nobody locks the door, and I can go in anywhere and also be thrown out anywhere. Does that answer your question?"

Grosz was hurt that the Germans had no interest in what he had painted during his twenty years in America, and remembered him only for his old social criticism. But in America, where his later work was better known, appreciation of it was also often denied him, especially during his last years. He was popular among his fellow artists because of his great personal magnetism and also because, by the 1950's, his reputation was that of a kind of Old Master. But many artists and critics never forgave him for having abandoned his earlier style. They felt he had committed the unforgiveable sin of Charlie Chaplin trying to play Hamlet. Some even saw in him a traitor who had sold out to that same "ruling class" he had once pilloried, and whose face he had now openly adopted. His recognition also suffered from the fact that he remained aloof from the abstract expressionists who had become the "ruling class" of American painters, and to whom Grosz' objectivity, his painstaking draftsmanship and insistence on recognizable and emotionally evocative subject-matter was anathema. Finally, as we have seen, Grosz' work in America was in many ways more Teutonic than what he had done in Germany when he owed so much to Daumier — and as Baur has noted, to many Americans "the Northern tradition has never been as sympathetic as that of France."

In brief, by the 1950's Grosz had become an outsider in America. And it was against the prevailing current that he had chosen to work. But with all this, the hatred and bitterness of his youth had given way to a compassion for all creatures. He had concentrated on topical and political targets. Now he reserved his fire for the archetypal ones, the timeless evils against which man has been pitted since the beginning of time. To him the victims of this evil were neither tragic nor comic; like Sisyphus, they were both. And when at the end they could no longer fight, they could at least hope to cultivate their garden.

After a second trip to Europe, Grosz decided to return to Germany for family reasons. The decision was hard. He was not tired of America, and he looked for-

27

ward to the three months he would spend each year at the Art Students League. While his house was emptied and the luggage packed, he took off — he did not want to witness his own farewell.

In May, just before he sailed, the American Academy of Arts and Letters presented him with its gold medal. Before a distinguished, respectful gathering, Grosz stood up to make his speech of acceptance. "Ladies and Gentlemen," he began in a resounding voice.[3] And then the microphone failed. While he continued to speak, making broad gestures and quite unaware of what had happened, the audience began to giggle; people assumed that the old jokester was doing a parody of the silent movies. The tragi-comic scene epitomized the last stage of his life and art; the means had failed by which he could bridge his loneliness. As a young man in Berlin, his mask had been that of a revolutionary; in his American maturity, his mask had been that of a suburban businessman — and both were the masks which a clown puts on to make his self-doubts laughable and hence bearable. Now Grosz had lost his protective masks, and he was about to lose the precious "little roots" which he had hoped would bind him to the American community. Like his Stickmen-heroes, he stood alone, with his rainbow banner in the world of grey — and the microphone, which civilization has created to heighten the audibility of the human voice and increase man's ability to communicate with his fellow men, sentenced Grosz to silence.

On May 27, 1959, he arrived in Berlin, "It is a fine thing that one has here — one has plenty of time," he said. On July 5 he met some friends in a *Weinstube;* in the early morning hours they took him home, unlocked the door of his house, bid him good night and left. He must have fainted then. Hours later, passers-by found him. He died without a word, while they were carrying him upstairs. He was sixty-six years old, and one of the great creative artists of our time.

RUTH BERENSON AND NORBERT MUHLEN

[1]Norman Rockwell, "My Adventures as an Illustrator," *Saturday Evening Post,* February 13, 1960, p. 112.

[2]*Art in Crisis,* Chicago, Henry Regnery, 1958.

[3]Grosz intended to deliver a speech based on his essay, "On My Drawings," which is published in full on p. 29 of this volume.

On my Drawings

Line does not exist in nature. Line is an invention of man; so, in fact, is all drawing. Line, drawing and writing are interrelated. The signature and the other descriptive material that often accompany the drawings of the old masters have no independent existence as writing, apart from the drawing itself; they form part of the whole conception. This idea is well illustrated in certain drawings of old masters like Dürer, Altdorfer and Mantegna. It is illustrated even more strikingly in Oriental drawings, where line and writing blend to form an indissoluble whole.

There must have been a reason for the invention of line. Yes, it is a guide for those who would venture into the formlessness that surrounds us on every side; a guide that leads us to the recognition of form and dimension and inner meaning. It is like the thread that Ariadne gave Theseus before he ventured into the mysterious recesses of the Labyrinth. Line guides us when we would enter the Labyrinth of the countless millions of natural objects that surround us. Without line we would soon be lost: never would we be able to find our way again out of the maze.

Let us then follow line withersoever it may go. It may lead to something quite definite and precise — a landscape, or a human face or figure. Or it may lead to the subconscious — the land of Fantasy, where fancy roams where it will.

Fantasy may be uninhibited fancy, which has no contact with the world of reality. But it may also lurk beneath a simple object in nature, like a tree or a rock or a sand dune. In fact it is almost everywhere if you can penetrate deeply enough beneath the husk of things. For, after all, nature is not simply the sum total of animate and inanimate objects. There is more to a tree or a rock or a sand dune than the mere outer appearance of reality. After many a prayer the angel might appear and perhaps the everlasting mystical truth hidden beyond our catalogue-minded general conception of nature. As the great Dürer once said: "Art is embedded in nature; he who can pluck it out possesses it."

The last century laid a great deal of emphasis on the outer world of reality but neglected the inner world. And so it is that to-day, when the search for inner truth again possesses the soul of man, we feel spiritually more akin to the painters of the Middle Ages than to the realistic draughtsmen who lived in the days of our grandfathers. A drawing by Pisanello or Grünewald is not a mere blueprint; it may be either sketchy or complete, but it will always be a spiritual organism.

Now line, as I have pointed out, is an invention — a product of the brain and soul of man. It is perfectly logical and natural, then, that to the lines that we find in nature we should add other lines that are the product of our inner vision. Such drawing can present both the outer husk and the inner essence. It is infinitely superior to the machine that we call the camera. You cannot take a camera with you into your dream world. No camera has ever been invented — or will be invented — that can give a flawless mechanical record of your day dreams or your inner visions.

From my early childhood days I liked to draw. Where did I draw? What media did I use? It matters little that I made my first drawings with white chalk on a blackboard and that later I did charcoal sketches after plaster casts at the Academy. The entire artistic life of a painter is a story of steady growth — of constant curiosity, observation and research. In the story of growth everything is significant, even the first faltering steps of artistic childhood. An artist's mature work often displays a certain adult naïveté.

The German painter Hans von Marées once said: "Drawings are only for the artist himself and, ultimately, for those to whom he has permitted the secret of his inner development to be revealed." For the general public a drawing without a story is uninteresting. This viewpoint ignores the underlying reality of a pure drawing — its function as an indicator of growth.

In this book I present for the first time to the public certain drawings of mine as a record of an artistic development. These drawings are

30

rather abstract in comparison with my earlier work, which was political and satirical. They are in different media. In part they present preliminary sketches for paintings. These display the result of study and research; they also display drawing for its own sake — drawing for the sheer pleasure of working with planes, lines, dots and hooks to represent textures, or blacks and whites, to conjure up sfumati *and* chiaroscuri.

You will note that, generally speaking, though I give free rein to my fancy, I have not neglected the outer shell of things. The utter rejection of reality is a perilous matter. Totally abstract fancy has a tendency to become stylized and conventional. Look for example at the drawings of Aubrey Beardsley, who had such a tremendous vogue around 1900, and you will see what I mean. Abstract fancy that becomes pure convention is as much to be shunned by the artist as the slavish copying of nature.

The searcher after Fantasy should not avoid reality; he should know how to present the outer appearance of things together with the inner content. The early Italian painters possessed this faculty to an exceptional degree. They created an inner world, yet left the exterior shell of reality intact.

I have always sought as models the various forms that nature takes; yet never did I approach the task with such zest and self-confidence as in America. I remember particularly the wonderful days I spent at Cape Cod in 1939.

Great cities had always fascinated me. I had felt the spell of huge towers with their myriads of human ants and termites, each engrossed in a tiny world of his own. I had felt the hidden joys and terrors and fears of urban life. I had been powerfully stirred by the great human drama which is a composite of these joys and sorrows. Yet Cape Cod offered me all this and more too. Here too were menace and sweetness and drama — the menace of hovering storm clouds and breaking waves, the sweetness of grass and sand and trees, the drama of ants, real ants, following the threads of their destiny amid the fantastically shaped dunes and the tall grasses.

In a Franciscan mood, I hobnobbed with trees and grasses and flowers. I made nature my friend and confidant in that wonderful year. I sat for hours on the dunes and observed and drew. I was filled with an inner calm and joy. My drawings reflected my mood; all my artistic production of that year was good. I was happy once more.

In the drawings I offer you in this book you will see the record of an artist's growth. In former days, when I essayed political and social satire, I often felt its limitations. In portraying and satirizing the events of the day, the comedies and tragedies of the passing scene, the artist is like a fiddler scraping on too small a violin. There is only a small place in great art for the quips and digs and innuendo of the satirist. In all humility I offer you the evidence that I have outgrown the satirical phase of my artistic development.

GEORGE GROSZ

Cape Cod, August 1944

32

Bibliography

BOOKS AND PORTFOLIOS

1917 *Erste George Grosz Mappe.* 9 Lithographien. Malik Verlag, Berlin.

Kleine George Grosz Mappe. 20 Lithographien. Malik Verlag, Berlin.

1919 *Das Gesicht der herrschenden Klasse.* 57 Zeichnungen. Malik Verlag, Berlin Halensee.

1920 *Gott mit Uns.* 9 Lithographien. Malik Verlag, Berlin.

Die Räuber. 9 Lithographien. Malik Verlag, Berlin.

HERZFELDE, WIELAND. *Tragigrotesken der Nacht. Träume.* 22 Zeichnungen. Malik Verlag, Berlin.

HUELSENBECK, RICHARD. *Phantastische Gebete.* Gedichte. 13 Zeichnungen. Malik Verlag, Berlin.

JUNG, FRANZ. *Die rote Woche.* Roman. 9 Lithographien. Malik Verlag, Berlin.

SCHOENLANK, BRUNO. *Sonniges Land. Kindergedichte.* 5 Zeichnungen und Aquarell. Paul Cassirer, Berlin.

1921 BALL, HUGO. *Flametti.* Gedichte. Reiss, Berlin.

DAUDET, ALPHONSE. *Tartarin von Tarascon.* Übersetzt von Klabund. Erich Reiss, Berlin.

George Grosz. 12 Drawings. Introduction by H. Simons. Musterbookhouse, Chicago.

Im Schatten. 9 Lithographien. Malik Verlag, Berlin.

HUELSENBECK, RICHARD. *Dr. Billig am Ende.* 8 Zeichn. Kurt Wolff, München.

JUNG, FRANZ. *Arbeitsfriede.* 6 Lithographien. Malik Verlag, Berlin.

MEYER, ALFRED RICHARD. *Munke Punke.* 6 Lithographien. F. Gurlitt. Dionysos, Berlin.

SINCLAIR, UPTON. *Hundert Prozent.* Roman. 10 Lithographien. Malik Verlag, Berlin.

WOLFRADT, WILLI. *George Grosz.* Mit 1 Farb. Titelbild und 32 Abb. (auf Tafeln). Klinkhardt & Biermann, Leipzig.

1922 ANDERSON NEXOE, MARTIN. *Die Passagiere der leeren Plätze.* 13 Abbildungen. Malik Verlag, Berlin.

FRIEDLAENDER, SALOMO (MYNONA). *George Grosz.* 27 Abb. R. Kaemmerer, Dresden.

Abrechnung folgt! 57 politische Zeichnungen. Malik Verlag, Berlin.

Ecce Homo. 84 Lithographien, 16 Aquarelle. Malik Verlag, Berlin.

KANEHL, OSKAR. *Steh auf Prolet!* Gedichte. 7 Abb. Malik Verlag, Berlin.

REIMANN, HANS. *Das Paukerbuch.* Satire. Paul Stegemann, Hannover.

REIMANN, HANS. *Sächsische Miniaturen.* Der Drache. Leipzig.

1923 *Mit Pinsel und Schere.* 9 Montagebilder. Malik Verlag, Berlin.

MEYER, ALFRED RICHARD. *Lady Hamilton.* 8 Lithographien. F. Gurlitt, Berlin.

1924 (1932) *Spiesser Spiegel.* 60 Zeichnungen (und ein Selbstbildnis). Reissner, Dresden.

MEYER, ALFRED RICHARD. *Munke Punke.* 8 Lithographien. F. Gurlitt, Berlin.

TAVOLATO, ITALO. *George Grosz.* 33 drawings. (text in Italian and English). Valori Plastici, Rome.

1925 FELS, FLORENT. *Propos d'artistes.* La Renaissance du Livre, Paris.

GROSZ, GEORGE UND WIELAND HERZFELDE. *Die Kunst ist in Gefahr; 3 Aufsätze.* Illustr. Malik Verlag, Berlin.

MANN, HEINRICH. *Kobes.* 10 Lithographien. Propyläen Verlag, Berlin.

ZUR MUEHLEN, HERMYNIA. *Was Peterchens Freunde erzählten.* Ein Märchen. 6 Zeichnungen. Malik Verlag, Berlin.

1926 BAZALGETTE, LÉON. *George Grosz. L'homme et l'oeuvre.* 26 illustrations. Les Ecrivains Réunis, Paris.

MAC ORLAN, PIERRE. *Port d'Eaux-Mortes.* 8 Lithographies. Au Sans Pareil, Paris.

TOLLER, ERNST. *Brokenbrow.* Trans. by Vera Mendel. 6 drawings. Nonesuch Press, London.

TOLLER, ERNST. *Hinkemann.* Tragedie. 6 dessins. Les Humbles, Paris.

1927 RAY, MARCEL. *George Grosz.* 40 illustr. G. Crès, Paris.

1928 *Hintergrund.* 17 Zeichnungen zur Aufführung des "Schwejk" in der Piscator Bühne. Malik Verlag, Berlin.

KANEHL, OSKAR. *Strasse Frei!* Der Spartakusbund, Berlin.

1929 AVERMAETE, ROGER. *George Grosz.* Arts et Metiers Graphiques, Paris.

Die Artisten. (1915-1917). Josef Portman, Litomysl (Czecoslovakia.)

1930 *Das neue Gesicht der herrschenden Klasse.* 60 Zeichnungen. Malik Verlag, Berlin.

Die Gezeichneten. 60 Zeichnungen. Malik Verlag, Berlin.

Ueber alles die Liebe. 60 Zeichnungen und Aquarelle. Bruno Cassirer, Berlin.

1931 DE LA ROCHELLE, DRIEU. *Music Hall.* Gallimard. Paris.

FRANZKE, GUENTHER. *Gesänge gegen bar.* Gedichte. 12 Zeichnungen. W. Jessen, Dresden.

A Post-war Museum. 28 drawings. Faber & Faber. London.

1932 BRECHT, BERTOLT. *Die drei Soldaten.* Gedicht. 25 Zeichnungen. G. Kiepenheuer, Potsdam.

KESTEN, HERMANN. *Glückliche Menschen.* Roman. G. Kiepenheuer, Potsdam.

PONS, PETER. *Der grosse Zeitvertreib.* Gedichte. 19 Zeichnungen. Mueller & Kiepenheuer, Potsdam.

1935 *Bagdad-on-the-Subway.* Six watercolors depicting O. Henry's New York. Print Club. (Portfolio.)

HENRY, O. *The Voice of the City and Other Stories.* 21 watercolors. Limited Editions Club, New York.

1936 *Interregnum.* 64 Lithographs. The Black Sun Press, New York.

1941 HECHT, BEN. *1001 Afternoons in New York.* Illustrated. 86 illustrations. Viking Press, New York.

1944 BARON, SYDNEY S. *One Whirl.* 26 illustrations. Lowell, New York.

DANTE. *The Divine Comedy.* 32 drawings. Modern Library, Random House, New York.

George Grosz Drawings. With an introduction by the Artist. H. Bittner and Co., New York.

35

George Grosz: 30 Drawings and Watercolors. Introduction by Walter Mehring. Erich S. Herrmann, New York.

MEHRING, WALTER. *No Road Back.* Poems. Frontispiece and 1 Illustration. Translated by S. A. De Witt. (Text in English and German.) S. Curl Inc., New York.

1945 MOLLINO, CARLO. *36 disegni di George Grosz.* 36 plates. Orma, Torino.

1946 BALLO, FERDINANDO, ed. *Grosz.* 57 illustrations. Documenti d'Arte Contemporaneo, Milano.

GROSZ, GEORGE. *A Little Yes and a Big No.* Transl. by Lola Sachs Dorin. With 272 Illustrations. Dial Press, New York.

1947 KESTEN, HERMANN. *Happy Man.* A Novel. Translated by Edward Crankshaw. J. Lane, London.

1948 HOFBAUER, IMRE, ED. *George Grosz.* 85 plates. Nicholson and Watson, London.

1955 ADE, WITBOI. *George Grosz.* (Mit einer Gesamtwürdigung des Künstlers von Walther G. Oschilewski.) 51 plates. Arani, Berlin.

Ein Kleines Ja und ein grosses Nein. Sein Leben von ihm erzählt. Rowohlt, Berlin.

Der Spiesser Spiegel. 60 Zeichnungen. Neue Auflage. Arani, Berlin. Grünewald.

CATALOGUES, PERIODICALS AND NEWSPAPERS

1916 *Almanach der Neuen Jugend für 1917.* 5 Zeichnungen. Verlag Neue Jugend, Berlin.

1916-17 HERZFELDE, WIELAND, ed. *Neue Jugend.* 8 Zeichnungen und 7 Gedichte von George Grosz. Verlag Neue Jugend, Berlin.

1918 DAÜBLER, THEODOR. George Grosz. *Neue Blätter für Kunst und Dichtung,* Jahrg. 1, pp. 153-4.

1919 GROSZ, GEORGE, ed. *Die Pleite, Jahrg.* 1 ff. Malik Verlag, Berlin-Leipzig.

1920 RAY, MARCEL. George Grosz. *Cahiers d'Aujourd'hui,* Paris, no. 1, Nov., pp. 27-33. (illustr.)

1921 WOLFRADT, WILLI. *George Grosz. Jahrb. der jungen Kunst,* Leipzig, Jahrg. 4, pp. 97-112. (illustr.)

1923 WESTHEIM. George Grosz Drawings. *Broom,* Rome, vol. 4, pp. 163-9. (illustr.)

1924 SCHEFFLER, KARL. George Grosz. *Kunst und Künstler,* Berlin, Jahrg. 22, pp. 182-6. (illustr.)

1926 Der Künstler als Journalist-George Grosz. *Kunst und Künstler,* Berlin Jahrg. 24, pp. 354-9. (illustr.)

1927 LANDAU, ROM. George Grosz. *Arts,* vol. 12, Dec., pp. 295-304. (11 illustr.)

SCHEFFLER, KARL. George Grosz: Ausstellung von Zeichnungen und Aquarellen im Verlag Bruno Cassirer. *Kunst und Künstler,* Berlin, Jahrg. 27, Apr. pp. 269-73. (5 illustr.)

El proceso al artista George Grosz. *Pluma,* Montevideo, vol. 13, Oct., pp. 90-99. (illustr.)

1930 BAZALGETTE, LÉON. George Grosz. *Chroniques du Jour,* Paris, vol. 4, Jul., p. 17-19. (illustr.)

Berliner Ausstellung. *Kunst und Künstler,* Berlin, Jahrg. 29, Dec., pp. 123-24.

TURKEL-DERI, FLORA. German Painter Not Guilty. *Art News,* vol. 29, Dec. 27, p. 9.

GROSZ, GEORGE. Lebenserinnerungen. *Kunst und Künstler,* Berlin, Jahrg. 29, Oct., Nov., pp. 15-22, 55-61. (18 illustr.)

1931 KIEN, WALTER. A German Caricaturist. *Nation,* vol. 132, Febr. 11, pp. 158-9.

BERTHELOT, P. Exposition. *Beaux-Arts,* Paris, vol. 9, Mar. (1 illustr.)

GEORGE, W. Art in Paris. *Formes,* Paris, no. 13, Mar. p. 52.

HOFMANN, H. Auseinandersetzung mit George Grosz. *Deutche Kunst und Dekoration,* Darmstadt, Jahrg. 67, Mar., p. 364.

GOODRICH, LLOYD. German Painting at the Museum of Modern Art. *Arts,* vol. 17, April, p. 506-7.

TURKEL-DERI, FLORA. Berlin Letter. *Art News,* vol. 30, Oct. 31, p. 22.

Grosz Acquitted of Blasphemy. *Art News,* vol. 30, Dec. 12, p. 7.

Exposition d'aquarelles et dessins. *Cahiers d'Art, vol. 6,* Paris, no. 2, p. 111.

German Painting and Sculpture. The Museum of Modern Art, New York, p. 23. (1 illustr.)

1932 PELIKAN, A. G. Lithographs by George Grosz. *Milwaukee Art Institute Bulletin,* vol. 5, Jan., p. 11.

Grosz and Sloan. *Art Digest,* vol. 6, April 15, pp. 4, 29-30.

Von Sternberg Buys Grosz's Married Couple. *Art Digest,* vol. 6, May 15, p. 8. (illustr.)

Art. *Time,* vol. 19, p. 20, June 20. (1 illustr.)

Grosz, of America. *Art Digest,* vol. 7, Oct. 15, p. 27.

Briefe aus Amerika. *Kunst und Künstler,* Berlin, Jahrg. 31, Aug., Aug.-Sept., Dec., pp. 273-8, 317-22, 433-43.

GROSZ, GEORGE. *Social Kunst,* Copenhagen, No. 9. 32 unnumbered pages. (28 illustr.)

1933 Barbizon Plaza Galleries Exhibition. *Art News,* vol. 31, March 18, p. 10.

MUMFORD, LEWIS. The Art Galleries. *New Yorker,* vol. 9, April 1, p. 38.

New York Criticism: Grosz Does Not Flatter America. *Art Digest,* vol. 7, April 1, p. 16.

Grosz "Slipping"? *Art Digest,* vol. 7, April 15, p. 32.

BENSON, E. M. George Grosz, Social Satirist. *Creative Art,* vol. 12, May, p. 340-7. (10 illustr.)

Exhibition of Drawings and Watercolors. *Milwaukee Institute Bulletin,* vol. 6, May, p. 2.

George Grosz: German Satirist. *Vanity Fair,* vol. 41, Nov., pp. 34-5. (4 illustr.)

1934 Exposition. *Beaux-Arts,* Paris, April 20, p. 6.

Grosz Exhibit held in Paris. *Art News,* vol. 32, May 26, p. 13.

Water-colours at the Mayor Gallery. *Apollo,* London, vol. 20, Aug., p. 107.

Notice biographique et bibliographique. *Amour de l'Art,* Paris, vol. 15, Oct., pp. 442-3, 445. (2 illustr.)

New York: Chameleon City. *Vanity Fair,* vol. 43, Nov., pp. 36-7. (10 illustr.)

1935 Grosz' "American Scene" Is Not Flattering. *Art Digest,* vol. 9, April 1, p. 8. (1 illustr.)

1936 What is so rare as a night in June? *Stage,* vol. 13, June, pp. 42-3.

SALPETER, HARRY. Caricature According to Grosz. *Ringmaster,* vol. 1, July-August, pp. 43-6. (5 illustr.)

BENÉT, WILLIAM ROSE. Grosz Lithographs. *Saturday Review of Literature,* vol. 15, Dec. 19, p. 14. (1 illustr.)

COWLEY, MALCOLM. Hymn of Hate (in "Books in Review"). *New Republic,* vol. 89, Dec. 23, pp. 249-50, (1 illustr.)

WHEELER, MONROE, ed. *Modern Painters and Sculptors as Illustrators.* The Museum of Modern Art, New York, p. 103. (1 illustr.)

1937 It Does Happen Here. *Art Digest,* vol. 11, April 15, p. 9.

1938 George Grosz — A Survey of His Art. *Chicago Art Institute Bulletin,* vol. 32, Dec., p. 112.

World-famed Artist Becomes U. S. Citizen. *Design,* vol. 40, Dec., sup. 2.

Grosz, American. *Art Digest,* vol. 13, Dec. 15, p. 15.

Exhibition of Twentieth Century German Art. *New Burlington Galleries,* London, pp. 16-17.

1939 Grosz Rated with Hogarth and Daumier. *Art Digest,* vol. 13, Jan. 1, p. 12. (1 illustr.)

George Grosz: First Complete View of a Satirist in Chicago. *Art News,* vol. 37, Jan. 7, pp. 8, 20. (2 illustr.)

Latest Work in Oil of a Celebrated German-American, Grosz (in "New Exhibitions of the Week.") *Art News,* vol. 37, March 25, p. 14.

Art. *Time,* vol. 33, March 27, p. 31. (1 illustr.)

DEVREE, HOWARD. Maynard Walker's Exhibition. *Magazine of Art,* vol. 32, Apr., pp. 234-5. (1 illustr.)

Grosz, Finding Security, Hangs up the Saber. *Art Digest,* vol. 13, April 1, p. 14. (1 illustr.)

Citizen or Artist? *Art Digest,* vol. 13, April 15, p. 7.

Grosz, Ex-German. *Art Digest,* vol. 14, Nov. 15, p. 17.

LOWE, JEANNETTE. Sand and Cloud Magic in Grosz's Cape Cod. *Art News,* vol. 38, Nov. 18, p. 22.

BARR, ALFRED H., JR., ed. *Art in Our Time.* The Museum of Modern Art, New York. (1 illustr.)

1940 BEMIS, MARION HOLDEN. Detroit Technical Workshop. *American Artist,* vol. 4, Oct., pp. 30-1.

RIESMAN, EVELYN T. After Seeing an Exhibition of the Work of George Grosz. *Twice a Year,* vol. 5-6, Fall 1940-Summer 1941, pp. 315-17.

1941 Drawings in California. *Art News,* vol. 40, Feb. 15, p. 7.

DORNER, ALEXANDER. Grosz: Post-War Pilgrim's Progress. *Art News,* vol. 40, April 15, pp. 25-6. (7 illustr.)

Nudes by Grosz. *Art Digest,* vol. 15, April 15, p. 9. (1 illustr.)

DEVREE, HOWARD New York Letter. *Magazine of Art,* vol. 34, April 19, pp. 207, 219-20. (1 illustr.)

BROWN, MILTON. *Death of an Artist* (in "Exhibitions: New York") *Parnassus,* vol. 13, May, p. 194. (1 illustr.)

Exhibition. *The Museum of Modern Art Bulletin,* vol. 9, Oct., pp. 13-14. (3 illustr.)

George Grosz from War to War. *Art Digest,* vol. 16, Oct. 15, p. 9. (1 illustr.)

COATES, ROBERT M. The Art Galleries. *New Yorker,* vol. 17, Oct. 25, pp. 4-5.

BRIAU, DORIS. Grosz in Retrospect (in "The Passing Show.") *Art News,* vol. 40, Nov. 1, p. 29. (1 illustr.)

European Artists in America. Addison Gallery of American Art, New York, pp. 22-27. (5 illustr.)

1942 Refugee Painter Shown. *Cincinnati Art Museum Bulletin,* no. 1, Feb., p. 8.

Retrospective Exhibition. *Milwaukee Art Institute Bulletin,* vol. 16, March, p. 2.

George Grosz, Artist. *Design,* vol. 43, May, p. 11. (1 illustr.)

George Grosz: Voice of Protest. *California Arts and Architecture,* vol. 59, June, (6 illustr.) pp. 20-1. (6 illustr.)

1943 BOSWELL, HELEN. Grosz Paints What He Can't Forget. *Art Digest,* vol. 17, Feb. 15, p. 7. (1 illustr.)

Associated American Artists Galleries Exhibition. *Art News,* vol. 42, Feb. 15, p. 23. (2 illustr.)

HERZFELDE, WIELAND. The Curious Merchant from Holland. *Harper's Magazine,* vol. 187, Nov., pp. 569-76.

BOYER, RICHARD O. Profiles. *New Yorker,* vol. 19, Nov. 27, pp. 32-6, 38, 41-4; Dec. 4, pp. 39-44, 46, 48; Dec. 11, pp. 37-42, 44. (3 illustr.)

Speaking of pictures: The Old Hell is Still Best. *Life,* vol. 15, Dec. 13, pp. 12-13, 15. (7 illustr.)

SOBY, JAMES THRALL and DOROTHY C. MILLER. *Romantic Painting in America.* The Museum of Modern Art, New York, pp. 41, 135. (1 illustr.)

1944 (George Grosz) Exhibition. *Baltimore Museum of Art News,* vol. 6, March, pp. 6-7.

American Paintings and Sculpture from the Museum's Collections. Newark Museum of Art Catalogue, pp. 54-5, 109.

WHEELER, MONROE, ed. *Modern Drawings.* The Museum of Modern Art, New York, p. 91. (2 illustr.)

1945 George Grosz Drawings. (Book Review.) *Art Digest,* vol. 19, Feb. 1, p. 29.

George Grosz: 30 Drawings and Watercolors, ed. by Walter Mehring. (Book Review.) *Art Digest,* vol. 19, Feb. 1, p. 29.

George Grosz Drawings. (Book Review.) *Art News,* vol. 44, Feb. 15, p. 24. (illustr.)

MIDDELDORF, ULRICH. George Grosz Drawings (in "Book Reviews.") *College Art Journal,* vol. 4, March, pp. 169-70.

SCHNIEWIND, CARL O. George Grosz Drawings (in "New Books.") *Magazine of Art,* vol. 38, April, pp. 154-6. (2 illustr.)

Six Painters: Paintings from the Encyclopaedia Britannica Collection. *American Artist,* vol. 9, Apr., p. 19. (1 illustr.)

Portrait. *Art Digest,* vol. 19, Apr. 1, p. 47.

O'CONNOR, JOHN, JR. Painting in the United States, 1945. *Carnegie Magazine,* vol. 19, Nov., pp. 140-1. (1 illustr.)

Portrait. *New York Times Magazine,* Nov. 4, p. 16.

Portrait. *Art Digest,* vol. 20, Dec. 15, p. 13.

1946 Gallery Vivienne Exhibition. *Art Digest,* vol. 20, Jun., p. 15.

COATES, ROBERT M. The Art Galleries. *New Yorker,* vol. 22, Oct. 19, pp. 62, 66-7.

FROST, ROSAMUND. Spotlight on George Grosz. *Art News,* vol. 45, Oct., pp. 50, 80. (2 illustr.)

MOLLINO, C. 36 disegni di George Grosz. *Emporium,* vol. 104, Oct., p. 188.

WOLF, BEN. Grosz Shocks a World Toward Peace. *Art Digest,* vol. 21, Oct. 15, p. 12. (2 illustr.)

Art. *Newsweek,* vol. 28, Oct. 21, pp. 106, 109. (1 illustr.)

PEARSON, R. M. Associated American Artists Galleries Exhibition. *Art Digest,* vol. 21, Nov. 1, p. 8.

Art. *Time,* vol. 48, Dec. 16, pp. 67-8. (2 illustr.)

GROSZ, GEORGE. *A Piece of My World in a World Without Peace.* Associated American Artists Galleries, New York.

1947 WILSON, EDMUND. Books. *New Yorker,* vol. 22, Jan. 4, pp. 65-6, 69-70.

TAUSON, H. W. Satirist's Dilemma. *Saturday Review of Literature,* vol. 30, Jan. 11, pp. 20-1. (2 illustr.)

REWALD, JOHN. A Little Yes and a Big No (in "Book Reviews.") *Magazine of Art,* vol. 40, Feb., pp. 81-2.

A Little Yes and a Big No. (Book Review.) *Art Digest,* Feb. 1, p. 27.

1948 LAUSFORD, ALONZO. Yes, We Have No Mananas. *Art Digest,* vol. 22, Apr. 15, p. 22. (1 illustr.)

George Grosz Watercolors at the Associated American Artists Galleries. *Art News,* vol. 47, May, p. 48. (1 illustr.)

SAHL, HANS, Die Stockmenshen. *Neue Zürcher Zeitung,* Zürich, May 7.

Portrait. *American Artist,* vol. 12, Sept., p. 26.

1949 GROSZ, GEORGE. I Teach Fundamentals. *College Art Journal,* vol. 9, No. 2, Winter 1949-50, pp. 199-201.

GRAFLY, DOROTHY. George Grosz. Painter and Prophet. *American Artist,* vol. 13, March, pp. 20-5, 64-5. (10 illustr.)

Exhibition at the Germanic Museum, Harvard University. *Art Digest,* vol. 24, Dec. 1, p. 13.

George Grosz, ed. by I. HOFBAUER. (Book Review.) *Studio,* vol. 138, Dec., p. 199. *Werk,* vol. 36, Dec., sup. p. 182.

PRASSE, L. E. George Grosz Lithograph: Storm Clouds, Cape Cod, 1949 Presentation Print of the Print Club of Cleveland. *Cleveland Museum of Art Bulletin,* vol. 36, Dec., pp. 195-6.

ROBINSON, AMY. Grosz Paints a Picture. *Art News,* vol. 48, Dec. pp. 35-7, 63. (8 illustr.)

WIGHT, FREDERICK S. *Milestones of American Painting in Our Century.* Institute of Contemporary Art, Boston, p. 86. (1 illustr.)

1952 Portrait. *American Artist,* vol. 16, May, p. 10.

Wine's better than acid. *Time,* vol. 60, Nov. 17, pp. 96-7.

Impressions of Dallas by George Grosz. Dallas Museum of Fine Arts Catalogue. (9 illustr.)

1953 DOLBIN, B. F. George Grosz, American Born in Germany. *Aufbau,* July 24.

GROSZ, GEORGE. Russlandreise 1922. *Der Monat,* Berlin, Jahrg. 5, no. 56, pp. 135-52. (7 illustr.)

1954 BAUR, JOHN I. H. *George Grosz.* Exhibition Catalogue. Whitney Museum of American Art, New York. (67 illustr.)

George Grosz by J. I. H. Baur. (Book Review.) *Canadian Art*, vol. 11, no. 4, p. 159.

Creative Process. *Art Digest*, vol. 28, Jan. 15, p. 16, 33. (2 illustr.)

DEVREE, HOWARD. Marin and Grosz. *New York Times*. Sec. 10, Sunday Jan. 17, p. 11.

GENAUER, EMILY. Art and Artists. *New York Herald Tribune*. Sec. 4, Sunday Jan. 17, p. 5.

Nothingness of Our Time. *Time*, vol. 63, Jan. 25, p. 90. (2 illustr.)

COATES, ROBERT M. The Art Galleries. *New Yorker*, vol. 29, Jan. 30, pp. 77-79. George Grosz Retrospective at the Whitney. *Art Student's League News*, January.

Associated American Artists Gallery Exhibition. *Art News*, vol. 52, Feb., p. 42.

McBRIDE, H. George Grosz: Becalmed Petrel. *Art News*, vol. 52, Feb., p. 27.

CHANIN, A. L. Profiteers and Prison Camps; full scale survey at the Whitney and small retrospective at AAA. *Art Digest*, vol. 28, Feb. 1, p. 12. (2 illustr.)

Whitney Museum Exhibition. *Art News*, vol. 53, March, p. 6. (4 illustr.)

KOROWICZ, DR. MAREK S. I Escaped to Speak for the Enslaved. *Life*, vol. 36, March 1, pp. 103-4; March 8, p. 128.

George Grosz by J. I. H. Baur. (Book Review.) *Art in America*, vol. 42, Oct. p. 231.

GROSZ, GEORGE. The Work of Oscar Fabrès. *Design and Paper*, no. 38. (Published by Marquardt and Co., Inc.)

SAHL, HANS. Die wechselnden Gesichter des George Grosz. *Almanach der Berliner Festwochen*, Berlin.

1955 George Grosz by J. I. H. Baur. (Book Review.) *Art Digest*, vol. 29, Jan. 15, p. 18.

Transformation of an Artist. *The London Times Literary Supplement*, Friday July 22.

Public Favorite: Grosz's "The Pit." *Time*, vol. 66, Nov. 21, pp. 94-95. (1 illustr.)

1958 Exhibition at New Art Center. *Art News*, vol. 57, Apr., p. 53.

1959 Selected by the National Institute of Arts and Letters to Receive the 1959 Gold Medal for Graphic Arts. *Arts*, vol. 33, March, p. 10.

Return of the Native, *Newsweek*, vol. 53, May 18, p. 70.

SAHL, HANS. Die Abschiedvorstellung der George Grosz. *Die Welt*, Hamburg, Jun. 3.

SAHL, HANS. Amerikas Abshied von George Grosz. Süddeutsche Zeitung, München. Jun. 5.

American Painting and Sculpture. American National Exhibition in Moscow, July 25-Sept. 5. Archives of American Art, Detroit. (Text in Russian.) (2 illustr.)

SEIBERLING, DOROTHY. The Last of a Master. *Life*, vol. 47, Jul. 27, p. 39.

Obituary. *Time*, vol. 74, Jul., p. 90.

George Grosz, 65, Noted Artist Dies. *New York Times*, Jul. 7.

OSCHILEWSKI, WALTER G. Ein grosser Moralist. Zum Tode von George Grosz. *Telegraf*, Jul. 7.

HUELSENBECK, RICHARD. Erinnerung an George Grosz. *Neue Zürcher Zeitung*, Zürich, Jul. 16.

KAHN, L. George Grosz zum gedenken. *Kunstwerk,* vol. 13, Aug., pp. 75-7. (3 illustr.)

KRAMER, H., Obituary. *Arts,* vol. 33, Sept., p. 13.

Obituary. *Current Biography,* vol. 20, Oct., p. 19.

RODITI, EDOUARD. Hannah Höch und die Berliner Dadaisten. *Der Monat,* Berlin, no. 134, Nov.

RODITI, EDOUARD. Interview with Hannah Höch on the Berlin Dadaist Group. *Arts,* vol. 34, Dec., pp. 24-9.

1960 Obituary *Current Biography Yearbook 1959,* p. 162.

RUTH BERENSON UND NORBERT MÜHLEN. George Grosz. *Der Monat,* Jahrg. 12, No. 141. pp. 20-32. June.

The following is a list of some of the periodicals in which just reproductions of Grosz' works appeared.

1929 *Beaux-Arts,* Paris, vol. 7, June, p. 28.

Graphischen Künste, Vienna, Jahrg. 56, July, p. 293.

Deutche Kunst und Dekoration, Darmstadt, Jahrg. 65, Oct., p. 30.

1930 *Der Cicerone,* Leipzig, Jahrg. 22, pt. 6, March, p. 167.

ditto, Jahrg. 22, pt. 8, Apr., p. 227.

1931 *Arts,* vol. 17, Apr., p. 503.

Art Digest, vol. 5, May 1, p. 7.

Creative Art Journal, vol. 8, June, p. 413.

Chicago Art Institute Bulletin, vol. 25, Sept., p. 83.

1932 *Deutsche Kunst und Dekoration,* Darmstadt, Jahrg. 69, Feb., p. 258.

Art Digest, vol. 6, Feb. 15, p. 20.

Creative Art Journal, vol. 11, Sept., p. 75.

ditto, vol. 11, Oct., p. 151.

1935 *American Magazine of Art,* vol. 28, Feb., p. 72.

ditto, vol. 28, May, p. 293.

1936 *Pennsylvania Museum of Art Bulletin,* vol. 31, March, p. 11.

American Magazine of Art, vol. 29, May, p. 336.

Prints, vol. 6, June, p. 243.

1937 *Art News,* vol. 35, May 1, p. 146.

Beaux-Arts, Paris, Oct. 15, p. 2.

Magazine of Art, vol. 38, Nov., sup. 7.

1938 *London Studio,* vol. 16 (Studio 116), Aug., p. 122.

Art Digest, vol. 12, Sept., p. 22.

Sept., p. 164.
London Studio, vol. 16 (Studio 116),

1939 *Magazine of Art,* vol. 32, Jan., p. 46.

Art News, vol. 37, Feb. 11, p. 6.

Art Digest, vol. 13, March 15, p. 27.

Fortune, vol. 20, no. 1, July, p. 144.

Coronet, vol. 7, Nov., p. 35.

Magazine of Art, vol. 32, Nov., p. 630.

ditto, vol. 32, Dec., p. 713.

1940 *Art Digest,* vol. 14, Feb. 1, p. 5.

Art News, vol. 38, Feb. 10, p. 8.

London Studio, vol. 19 (Studio 119), May, p. 159.

Magazine of Art, vol. 33, May, p. 285.

Art Digest, vol. 14, May 1, p. 12.

Art News, vol. 38, May 11, p. 9.

ditto, vol. 38, May 18, p. 7.

Art Digest, vol. 15, Dec. 1, p. 5.

1941 *London Studio*, vol. 22 (Studio 122), Jan. 1, p. 21.

Art News, vol. 39, Jan. 25, p. 14.

Magazine of Art, vol. 34, Feb., p. 90.

ditto, vol. 34, April, p. 207.

Art News, vol. 40, Oct. 15, p. 19.

ditto, vol. 40, Nov. 1, p. 13.

Harvard University. Fogg Art Museum Bulletin, vol. 9, Nov., p. 106.

Magazine of Art, vol. 34, Nov., pp. 488-9.

Fortune, vol. 24, no. 6, Dec., p. 113.

1942 *Art News*, vol. 41, Feb. 15, p. 12.

ditto, vol. 41, April 1, p. 16.

Art Digest, vol. 16, April 1, p. 9.

Art News, vol. 41, May 15, p. 21.

Magazine of Art, vol. 35, Nov., p. 246.

ditto, vol. 35, Dec., p. 282.

1943 *Fortune*, vol. 27, no. 1, Jan., p. 79.

Art News, vol. 41, Feb. 1, p. 21.

Art Digest, vol. 18, Oct. 15, p. 7.

1944 *London Studio*, vol. 27, (Studio 127), June, p. 177.

1945 *Magazine of Art*, vol. 38, April, pp. 154-5.

Art Digest, vol. 19, April 1, p. 42.

ditto, vol. 20, Oct. 15, p. 5.

Art News, vol. 44, Oct. 15, p. 11.

Carnegie Magazine, vol. 19, Nov., p. 140.

1946 *American Artist*, vol. 10, Jan., p. 14.

Emporium, Jahrg. 103, April, p. 202.

Magazine of Art, vol. 39, Nov., p. 320.

1947 *American Artist*, vol. 11, Jan., p. 31.

Art News, vol. 46, April, p. 33.

Arts, August 1, p. 1.

Milwaukee Gallery of Art Notes, vol. 20, Oct., p. 5.

1948 *Art News*, vol. 47, Oct., p. 25.

Studio, vol. 136, Dec., p. 197.

1949 *Fortune*, vol. 39, no. 2, Feb., p. 118.

Print Collector's Quarterly, vol. 30, June, p. 30.

1951 *Art News Annual*, vol. 21, p. 146.

1952 *Art News*, vol. 51, May, p. 26.

Magazine of Art, vol. 45, Nov., p. 311.

1953 *The Museum of Modern Art Bulletin*, vol. 20, no. 3-4, p. 28.

1954 *American Artist*, vol. 18, April, p. 42.

1955 *Art Digest*, vol. 29, Jan. 15, p. 18.

Print, vol. 9, May, p. 20.

1956 *College Art Journal*, vol. 15, no. 3, p. 271.

1957 *Artist*, vol. 53, Sept., p. 132.

Art News, vol. 56, Nov., p. 43.

Studio, vol. 154, Nov., p. 137.

1958 *The Museum of Modern Art Bulletin*, vol. 25, no. 4, p. 7.

1960 *Art in America*, vol. 48, no. 2, Summer, p. 36.

Catalogue of Plates

The dimensions, which are sheet size, are given in inches, height preceeding width. Whenever possible, note has been made of whatever writing is by the artist himself in order to identify fully the works reproduced. Note of signature, date, or inscription in parentheses indicates that they appear on the original but have been omitted from the reproduction for technical reasons. When not otherwise stated, works which form part of Ecce Homo *are reproduced directly from the first edition of* Ecce Homo, *published in Berlin in 1922 by Malik Verlag; works which form part of* Interregnum *are reproduced from the first edition of* Interregnum, *published in New York in 1936 by The Black Sun Press. When the source is not mentioned, the works reproduced belonged to the artist as late as 1944 after which time we have no definite record of their whereabouts.*

The order of the plates is roughly chronological, with the color plates divided throughout the book and in chronological order among themselves.

BLACK and WHITE

1 SUBURB OF BERLIN. 1911. Pencil. 5⅛ x 10 9/16. Signed: Grosz. Page from a sketchbook. Estate of the Artist.

2 HELGOLAND. 1911. Pencil. 6¼ x 8⅜. Estate of the Artist.

3 PANDEMONIUM AUGUST 1914. 1914. Pen and ink. 19¾ x 12½. Signed and dated: Grosz 1914. Collection Bernard J. Reis, New York.

4 STREET CORNER. 1915. Lithograph. 19 x 13¾. Signed and dated: Grosz 1915. Estate of the Artist.

5 ACROBATS. 1915. Pen and ink. Signed: Grosz. *Ecce Homo*, pl. 50.

6 CLOWNS AND DOGS. 1915. 11 3/16 x 8⅞. Signed: Grosz. Estate of the Artist.

7 MURDER. 1916. Pen and ink. Signed: Grosz. *Ecce Homo*, pl. 12.

8 SEX MURDER IN THE ACKERSTRASSE. 1916. Pen and ink. Signed: Grosz. *Ecce Homo*, pl. 32.

9 REAR BUILDING FOUR FLIGHTS UP. 1916. Pen and ink. (Signed: Grosz). *Ecce Homo*, pl. 49.

10 APACHES (AFTER IT WAS OVER THEY PLAYED CARDS). 1916. Pen and ink. 9⅜ x 12. Signed: Grosz. *Ecce Homo*, pl. 58.

11 CAFÉ. 1916. Pen and ink. (Signed: Grosz). *Ecce Homo*, pl. 41.

12 SUBURB. 1916. Pen and ink. Signed: Grosz. *Ecce Homo*, pl. 73.

13 PEDESTRIANS. 1917. Pen and ink. 11 7/16 x 8⅞. Estate of the Artist.

14 DEDICATED TO FRANZ JUNG. 1917. Pen and brush. Signed: Grosz. *Ecce Homo*, pl. 46.

15 THE END. 1917. Pen and brush. Signed: Grosz. *Ecce Homo*, pl. 83.

16 THE WHITE SLAVE TRADER. ca. 1917. Watercolor. Signed: Grosz. *Ecce Homo*, pl. VIII.

17 FURLOUGH. 1917. Watercolor. 18¼ x 13⅝. Signed: Grosz. *Ecce Homo*, pl. I.

18 FRIEDRICHSTRASSE. 1918. Pen and ink. Signed: Grosz. *Ecce Homo*, pl. 1.

19 EVA. 1918. Pen and ink. Signed: Grosz. *Ecce Homo*, pl. 51.

20 HOMEWORK (Self-portrait). 1917-1918. Pen and ink. 23⅛ x 14 3/16. Signed: Grosz. Collection Kate Steinitz, Los Angeles, California.

21 FIT FOR ACTIVE SERVICE (K.V.). 1918. Pen and brush. 20 x 14⅜. Signed: George Grosz. Collection The Museum of Modern Art, New York. A. Conger Goodyear Fund.

22 BEAUTY PARADE IN MOTZSTRASSE. 1918. Pen and ink. *Ecce Homo*, pl. 7.

23 THE POSSESSED FORESTER'S ASSISTANT. 1918. Pen and ink. *Ecce Homo*, pl. 24.

24 REMEMBER (In memory of Rosa Luxemburg and Karl Liebknecht). 1919. Pen and brush. 24 x 16. (Signed: Grosz). *Interregnum*, pl. 35. Collection Erich Cohn, New York.

25 THE WHITE GENERAL. 1919. Pen and ink. 22¼ x 20½. Signed: Grosz. Collection Erich Cohn, New York.

26 CROSS-SECTION. 1920. Pen and ink. Signed: Grosz. *Ecce Homo*, pl. 68.

27 SEPARÉ. 1920. Pen and ink. 25¾ x 17. Signed, and dated: Grosz (1920). Caption: Im Separee. Early version for *Ecce Homo*, pl. 22. Estate of the Artist.

28 TRIO. 1919. Pen and ink. Signed: Grosz. *Ecce Homo*, pl. 74.

29 DAY OFF. 1921. Pen and crayon. (Signed: Grosz). *Ecce Homo*, pl. 81.

30 REPUBLICAN AUTOMATONS. 1920. Watercolor. 23⅝ x 18⅝. Collection The Museum of Modern Art, New York. Advisory Committee Fund.

31 THE ENGINEER HEARTFIELD. 1920. Watercolor and collage. 16 x 11¼. Collection The Museum of Modern Art, New York. Gift of General A. Conger Goodyear.

32 THE RESPONSIBLE ONES. 1920. Pen and ink. (Signed: Grosz). *Ecce Homo*, pl. 23.

33 GRIM MAN. 1918. Pen and ink. Signed: Grosz. *Ecce Homo*, pl. 4.

34 THE UNCLE. ca. 1921. Pen and ink. 24½ x 18⅜. Signed: Grosz. Collection Erich Cohn, New York.

35 A CHARACTER. 1921. Pen and ink. Signed: Grosz. *Ecce Homo*, pl. 15.

36 CAFÉ. 1922. Pen and ink. 12⅜ x 25½. Collection The Museum of Modern Art, New York. Lillie P. Bliss Bequest.

37 MAN AND WOMAN. ca. 1920 Pencil. 7 x 4 7/16 (actual size). Signed: Grosz. Page from a sketchbook. Estate of the Artist.

38 BERLIN STREET SCENE. 1920. Pen and ink. 20¾ x 14. Signed, dated, and inscribed: Grosz 1920 / Berlin. From *Ecce Homo*. Collection The Metropolitan Museum of Art, New York. Gift of Priscilla A. B. Henderson, 1950.

39 UNION OFFICERS AT WORK. ca. 1922. Pen and ink. 26¾ x 16⅞. Caption: Gewerkschaftssekretäre bei der Arbeit. Estate of the Artist.

40 GAUDEAMUS IGITUR. 1922. Pen and ink. (Signed: Grosz). *Ecce Homo*, pl. 52.

41 THE COMING GENERATION. 1922. Pen and brush. (Signed: Grosz). *Ecce Homo*, pl. 19.

42 QUARTETT. 1922. Pen and ink. 18⅛ x 23⅝. On reverse side: 53 Guvlitt. Estate of the Artist.

43 LIVED FOR NOTHING II. ca. 1922. Pen and ink. 23 5/16 x 18⅛. Caption: umsonst gelebt II. On reverse side: drawing of a soldier. Estate of the Artist.

44 THE PEOPLE HAVE WON. ca. 1924. Pen and ink. 19 15/16 x 16⅜. Caption: Das Volk hat gesiegt. On reverse side: drawing of four figures. Estate of the Artist.

45 BLIND MAN. 1923. Pencil. 23½ x 18. Signed and dated: Grosz 1923.

46 THE GENERALS. 1924. Pen and ink. 25½ x 19¼. Signed: Grosz. Collection Erich Cohn, New York.

47 STORES IN A SUBURB. 1926. Pen and ink. 24⅝ x 17¾. Signed and dated: Grosz 1926. Estate of the Artist.

48 THERE'S STILL SANTA CLAUS. ca. 1926. Pen and ink. Signed: Grosz. *Interregnum*. pl. 24.

49 A LITTLE LOVE SONG. ca. 1926. Pen and ink. Signed: Grosz. *Interregnum*, pl. 34.

50 FORECLOSURE. ca. 1928. Pen and ink. Signed: Grosz. *Interregnum*, pl. 31.

51 CHRIST WITH THE GAS MASK. 1927-1928. Pen and ink. 20 x 15. Signed: Grosz. Collection Erich Cohn, New York.

52 PORTRAIT OF ANNA PETER. 1926-1927. Pencil. 26⅝ x 21. Signed: Grosz. Collection The Museum of Modern Art, New York. Gift of Paul J. Sachs.

53 CANIS-SUR-MER, FRANCE. 1927. Pen and ink. 18⅞ x 24¾. (Signed, dated, and inscribed: Grosz/ Canis s. mer/ 1927/ France). On reverse side: drawing of two figures. Estate of the Artist.

54 CHEZ EMILE HASENBOHLER. 1927. Pen and ink. 18¾ x 24¾. (Signed, dated, and inscribed: 10 Hier sitst man gut/Grosz/ Paris 27/Chez Emile Hasenbohler). On reverse side: drawing of five figures. From *Uber alles die Liebe*. Estate of the Artist.

55 PORTRAIT OF MAX HERRMANN-NEISSE. 1927. Pencil. 21½ x 18½. Signed, dated, and inscribed: The Poet Max Herrmann-Neisse died in exile in London/ done about 1927 as a study for my portrait/ to Erich and Lene Cohn in old friendship/ George Grosz/Douglaston 1941. Collection Erich Cohn, New York.

56 LAST CALL. 1931. Pen and ink. 23⅝ x 18. Signed: Grosz. Illustration for *Three Soldiers*, by Bert Brecht. Collection Erich Cohn, New York.

57 HAPPY INSANITY. ca. 1933. Pen and ink. 25 9/16 x 20⅝. Estate of the Artist.

58 BEER HALL NO. 23. 1933. Pen and ink. 26 x 19¾. Signed: Grosz. (Inscription: 23 Stehbierhalle/Meinen lieben Robert Keller herzlich George 1933). On reverse side: Cancelled ink drawing of crowd in city street carrying American flags blasted by falling bombs/ No. 23 Stehbierhalle. Collection The Baltimore Museum of Art, Baltimore, Maryland.

59 A LITTLE CHILD SHALL LEAD THEM. 1934-1935. Pen and ink. Signed: Grosz. *Interregnum*, pl. 8.

60 FIFTEEN POUNDS UNDERWEIGHT. 1935. Pen and ink. Signed: Grosz. *Interregnum*, pl. 18.

61 IN CONFERENCE (THINGS MIGHT BE WORSE). ca. 1933. Pen and ink on tan paper. 18⅝ x 24⅝. Signed: Grosz. On reverse side:

27/Business Talk/ Friends (crossed out.) Stamped: B. A. *Interregnum*, pl. 13. The Baltimore Museum of Art, Baltimore, Maryland. Gift of Miss Blanche Adler.

62 THAT'LL LEARN 'EM. 1935. Pen and ink. Signed: Grosz. *Interregnum*, pl. 41.

63 THE LEISURE CLASS. 1935. Pen and ink. Signed: Grosz. *Interregnum*, pl. 47.

64 A WRITER, IS HE? 1935. Pen and ink. (Signed: Grosz). *Interregnum*, pl. 45.

65 AFTER THE QUESTIONING. 1935. Watercolor. 17¼ x 22¾. Signed and dated: Grosz 1935. Pen and ink version in *Interregnum*, pl. 51. Collection Arnott J. White, New York.

66 THE AMBASSADOR OF GOOD WILL. 1936. Watercolor. 18 x 24. Signed and dated: Grosz '36. Caption: The Ambassador of

Good Will. Collection The Metropolitan Museum of Art, New York. Gift of Priscilla A. B. Henderson, 1950.

67 EVICTION. ca. 1935. Pen and ink. (Signed: Grosz). *Interregnum*, pl. 30.

68 FINIS. ca. 1935. Pen and ink. Signed: Grosz. *Interregnum*, pl. 64.

69 ROCKS AND FERNS AT BORNHOLM. 1935. Pen and ink. 15½ x 19⅜. Signed: Grosz.

70 PEASANT WAGON. ca. 1935. Pen and ink. 9 x 12. Caption: 11 Bauernwagen. Study for *Interregnum*, pl. 19. Page from a sketchbook. Estate of the Artist.

71 MARTIN WITH THE MUMPS. 1935. Pencil. 18 x 23⅛. Signed, dated, and inscribed: Grosz 35/ Bayside Lg Island/My son Martin in bed with mumps.

72 PETER READING. 1936. Charcoal. 25 x 19. Signed, dated, and inscribed: Peter/Grosz 36/Douglaston/Peter reading.

73 DRAPED DUMMY. 1936. Charcoal. 25 x 19. Signed, dated, and inscribed: Grosz (36/ Douglaston). Private Collection, Pasadena, California.

74 AUNT BETTY. 1935. Pencil. 25 x 19. Signed, dated, and inscribed: Grosz/Portrait study/ For my dear Erich for his forthcoming birthday to remember the sitting for 2 portraits/ July 6/George. Collection Erich Cohn, New York.

75 TORSO. ca. 1935. Pencil. 19 11/16 x 15 7/16. Estate of the Artist.

76 TWO NUDES. ca. 1936. Pencil. 25 x 19. Signed and inscribed: Grosz/Dr 7 studies. Estate of the Artist.

77 TWO NUDES. 1936. Pen and green ink on tracing paper. 16⅞ x 13⅞. Estate of the Artist.

78 SNOW WHITE AND THE SEVEN DWARFS. ca. 1934. Pen and ink. 18⅞ x 24 11/16. Signed and inscribed: Grosz (11 Snowhite & the 7 dwarfs). Estate of the Artist.

79 HANSEL AND GRETEL. ca. 1934. Pen and ink. 19 x 24⅞. Signed and inscribed: Grosz/8 Hansel & Gretel). Estate of the Artist.

80 ONCE UPON A TIME. 1936. Pen and ink. Signed, dated, and inscribed: Grosz 36/ Bayside. *Interregnum*, pl. 7.

81 EVEN MUD HAS AN END. 1936. Pen and ink. (Signed: Grosz). Study for "The Wanderer." *Interregnum*, pl. 4.

82 NO LET UP. 1936. Pen and ink. Signed: Grosz. *Interregnum*, pl. 63.

83 STUDY FOR A PAINTING. 1937. Pencil. 25 x 19. Signed and dated: George Grosz 37. Collection Norbert Muhlen.

84 TWO NUDES. 1936. Charcoal. 24½ x 18½. Signed: Grosz. Collection Maria Bittner, New York.

85 FLOWERS. 1937. Pen and ink. 19¾ x 15½. Signed, dated, and inscribed: Helene Cohn mit Allerherzlichstem Glückwunsch z. Geburts Tage Sept 6 1937 George Grosz. Collection Erich Cohn, New York.

86 THE RIDER OF THE APOCALYPSE (I WAS ALWAYS PRESENT). 1936. Pen and ink. 22¼ x 17⅛. Signed: Grosz. Signed, dated and inscribed on reverse side: George Grosz/202 Shore Road/ Lg Island/ 18 from *Interregnum*/ Chicago/The Rider is loose again/ 1936. Collection Erich Cohn, New York.

49

87 SAILOR AND GIRL. 1933. Watercolor. 19 x 26⅛. Signed, dated, and inscribed: To Ernest the wonderful friend and neighbor always/George/Feby 54. Collection Ernest B. Ashton, Huntington, Long Island.

88 BOWERY, NEW YORK. 1934. Watercolor. 26 x 19. Signed, dated, and inscribed: Bowery/ New York/Grosz 1954/ Bayside L. Island. Collection Walter Herlinger, New York.

89 TREES AT TRURO, CAPE COD. 1939. Pen on reddish paper. 20 x 14.

90 STUDY IN TEXTURE. 1939. Chalk and sanguine. 25 x 19. Signed and dated: Grosz 39.

91 DUNES AND MIST, CAPE COD. 1939. Pencil. 15½ x 19½. Signed and dated: Grosz 39.

92 SAND DUNES, CAPE COD. 1939. Chalk. 13½ x 16⅝.

93 NUDE. 1940. Oil on canvas. 21¼ x 16½. Signed, dated, and inscribed on the back: 1. red priming/Indian Red and Egg tempera/2. medium-DAMAR in terpentine/ 3. all Gil paints/George Grosz pictor/ Douglaston 1940/November. Collection Adolph Tausik, New York.

94 STUDY AFTER RUBENS. 1939. Charcoal. 25 x 19. Signed, dated, and inscribed: Herbert Bittner to remember OVER LAND & MEER/Douglaston 1942/ George Grosz after Rubens/Grosz 39.

95 WOMAN UNDRESSING. 1940. Pencil, chalk, and watercolor. 23 x 15½.

96 PORTRAIT OF WALTER MEHRING. 1945. Charcoal on blue paper. 25 x 18⅜. Signed, dated, and inscribed: George Grosz/Walter Mehring/April 1945/Douglaston. Estate of the Artist.

97 NUDE TORSO. 1950-1951. Pencil. 9¾ x 5 5/16. Signed: Grosz. Page from a sketchbook. Fogg Art Museum, Harvard University, Cambridge, Massachusetts. Paul J. Sachs Collection.

98 NUDE. 1945. Pencil on pink paper. 18¼ x 23⅛. Signed: Grosz. Estate of the Artist.

99 NUDE. 1945. Pencil. 18⅞ x 23⅞. Signed and dated: Grosz 45. Estate of the Artist.

100 PINE TREES, CAPE COD. 1939. Watercolor. 15⅜ x 19⅜. Signed, dated, and inscribed: Grosz 39/Truro. Collection The Metropolitan Museum of Art, New York. Arthur H. Hearn Fund, 1939.

101 PEACE II. 1946. Oil on canvas. 47 x 33¼. Collection Whitney Museum of American Art, New York.

102 TRAPPED MOUSE. 1950-1951. Pencil. 9¼ x 6. Signed: Grosz. Page from a sketchbook. Fogg Art Museum. Anonymous gift in gratitude for the friendship of Dean Wilbur Joseph Bender.

103 TRAPPED MOUSE. 1950-1951. Pencil. 9¼ x 6. Signed: Grosz. Page from a sketchbook. Fogg Art Museum. Anonymous gift in gratitude for the friendship of Dean Wilbur Joseph Bender.

104 SKETCH OF A MOUSE. 1950-1951. Pencil. 9¼ x 6. Signed: Grosz. Page from a sketchbook. Fogg Art Museum. Anonymous gift in gratitude for the friendship of Dean Wilbur Joseph Bender.

105 TWO MICE. 1950-1951. Pencil 9¼ x 6. Signed: Grosz. Page from a sketchbook. Fogg Art Museum. Anonymous gift in gratitude for the friendship of Dean Wilbur Joseph Bender.

106 HOPE OF LIBERATION. 1953. Pen and wash. Signed: Grosz. Commissioned by LIFE Magazine for the March 8, 1954 issue. Courtesy LIFE Magazine.

107 RUSSIA'S FACELESS LEGIONS. 1953. Pen and wash. Signed: Grosz. Commissioned by LIFE Magazine for the March 1, 1954 issue. Courtesy LIFE Magazine.

108 WAVING THE FLAG. 1947-1948. Watercolor. 25 x 18. Signed Grosz. Collection Whitney Museum of American Art, New York.

COLOR PLATES

BERLIN CAFÉ. ca. 1928. Watercolor. 25 x 18. Collection Arnott J. White. *Facing page 52.*

THE RIDER OF THE APOCALYPSE. (I WAS ALWAYS PRESENT). 1942. Oil on canvas. 36 x 28. Signed and inscribed on the back: I, I was always present/ George Grosz pinx./Douglaston Lg. I. Collection Galleries of Cranbrook Academy of Art, Bloomfield Hills, Michigan. Photograph: Harvey Croze. *Facing plate 18.*

THE WANDERER. 1943. Oil on canvas. 30 x 40. Collection Rochester Memorial Art Gallery, Rochester, New York. *Facing plate 35.*

THE PIT. 1946. Oil on canvas. 60¼ x 37¼. Wichita Art Museum, Wichita, Kansas, Roland P. Murdock Collection. *Facing plate 52.*

ENEMY OF THE RAINBOW. 1947-1948. Watercolor. 26¼ x 19. Signed: Grosz. Estate of the Artist. *Facing plate 72.*

OLD MAN WATERING FLOWERS. 1958. Watercolor. 19¼ x 15¼. Signed: Grosz. Collection Dr. William N. Young, Halesite, Long Island. *Facing plate 89.*

1

2

3

9

10

11

14

15

16

17

19

20

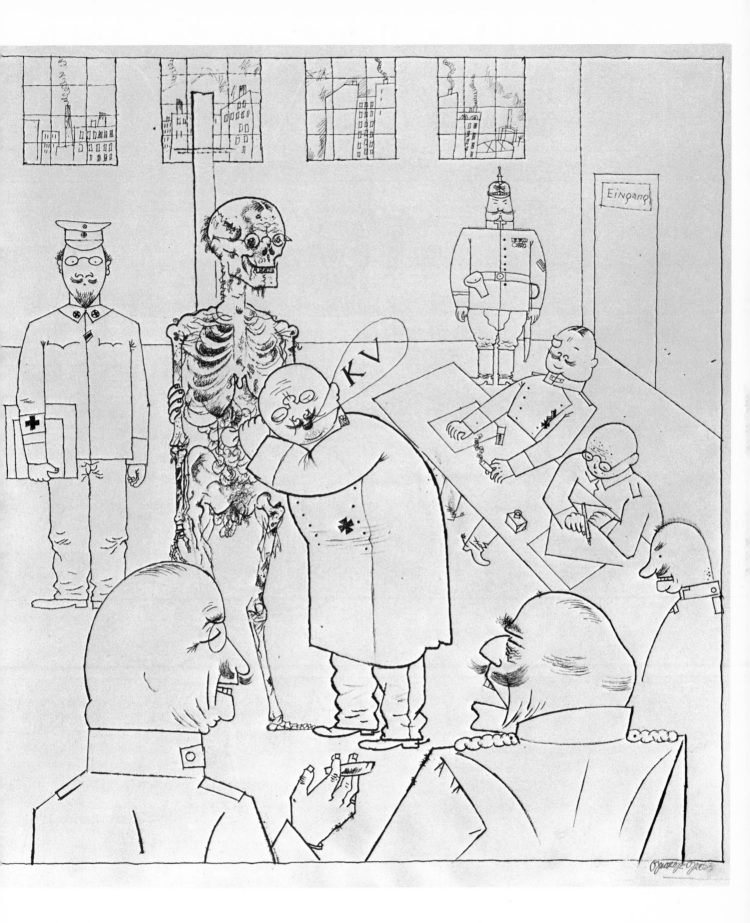

21

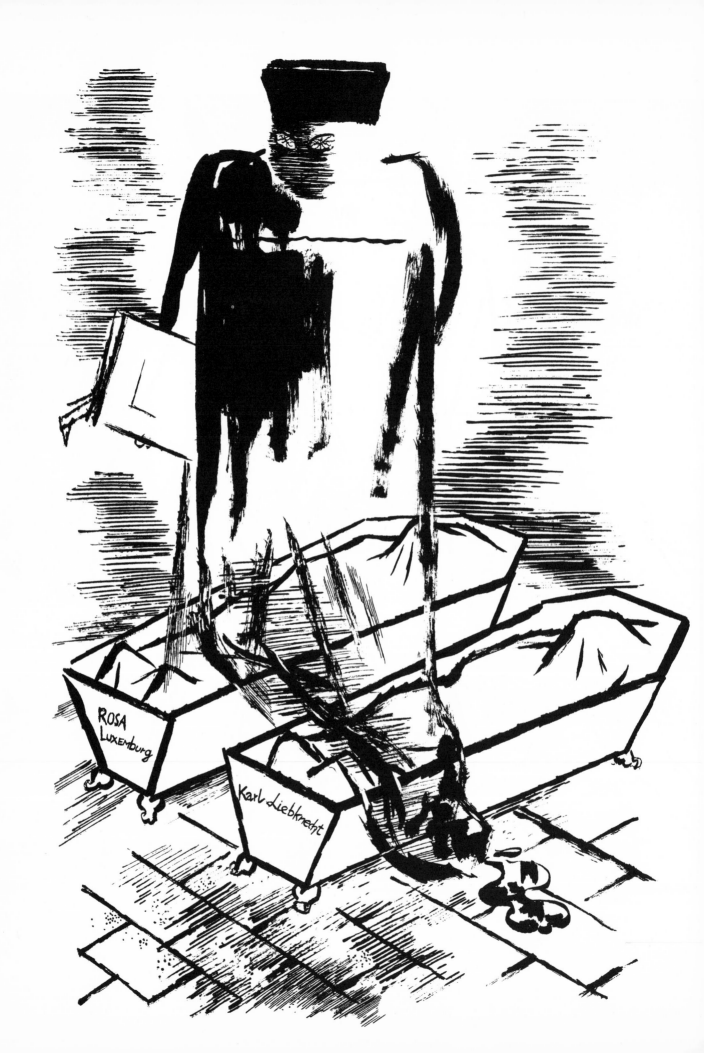

24

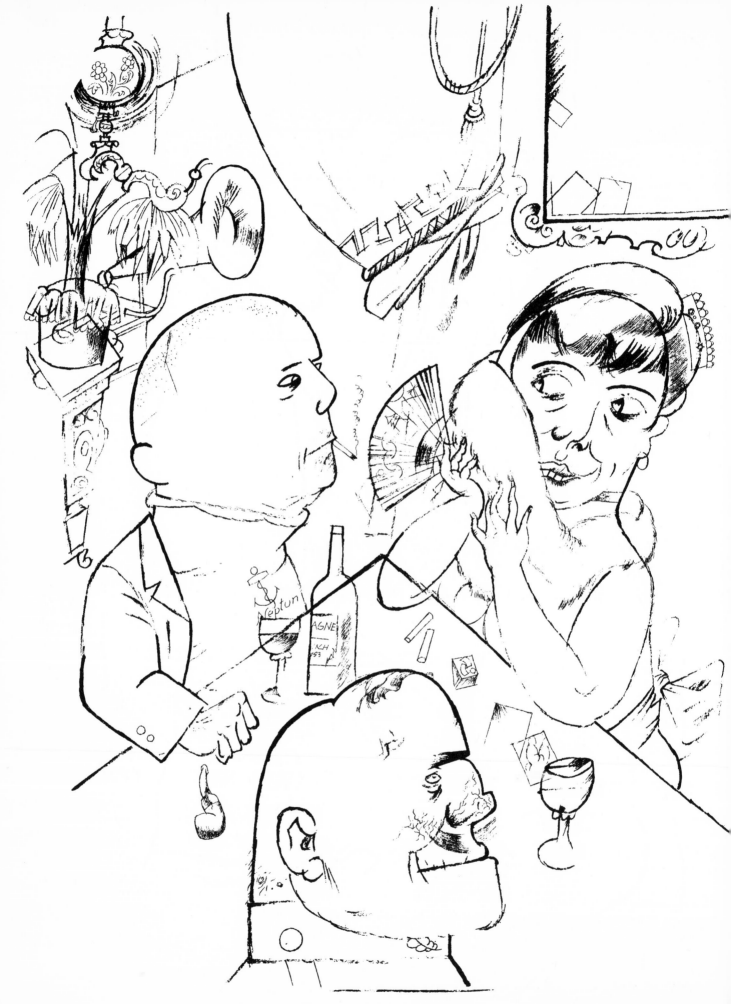

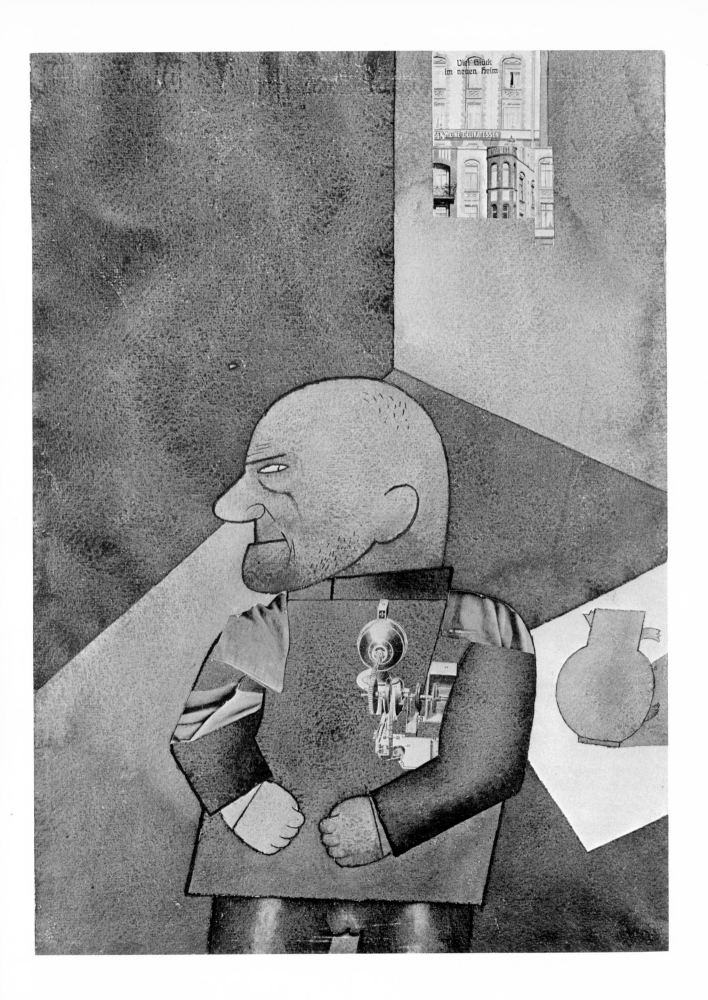

31

33

34

37

38

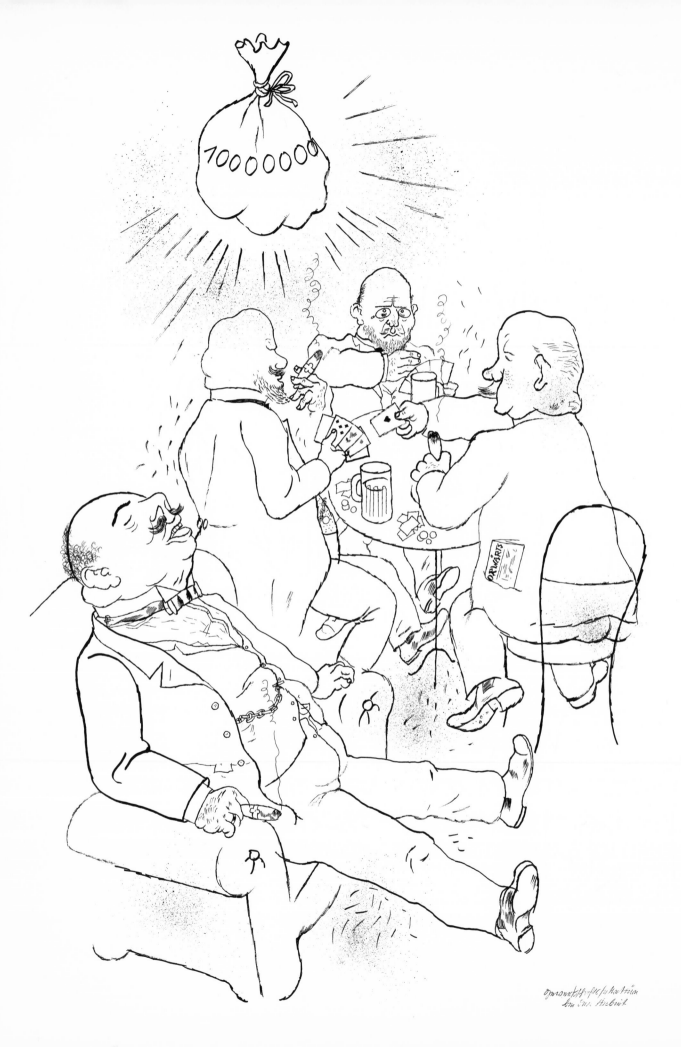

41

umsont gelebt II

43

Das Volk hat gesiegt

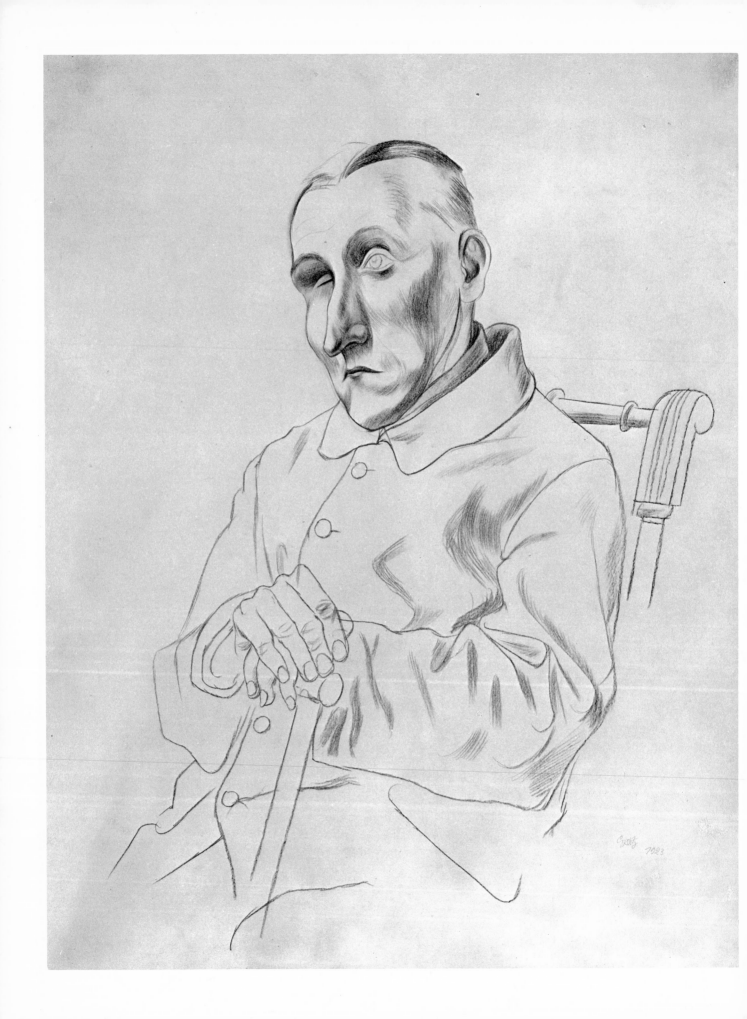

45

Der beliebte
Haarschneidestuhl
für Kinder

Damen
und
Herren
Frisör

HÖHENSONNE
Original Hanau 0,50

Reiss
Abbau

Anfertigung
sämtlicher
Hauptfrau

Adolf Becker

Herren Moden

ROYAL HENNA
Die Weltharfarbe

Fromms
Vanishing
Cream

Fromms

SIMI

HA
Fab

Bubikopf schneiden
frisieren in jeder
gewünschten Art

GROSZ
1926

53

54

The poet Max Herrmann-Neisse
died in exile in London
late about 1927 as study for my portrait
to Eddie X Zone Eberts
in old friendship
George Grosz
Douglaston 1944

58

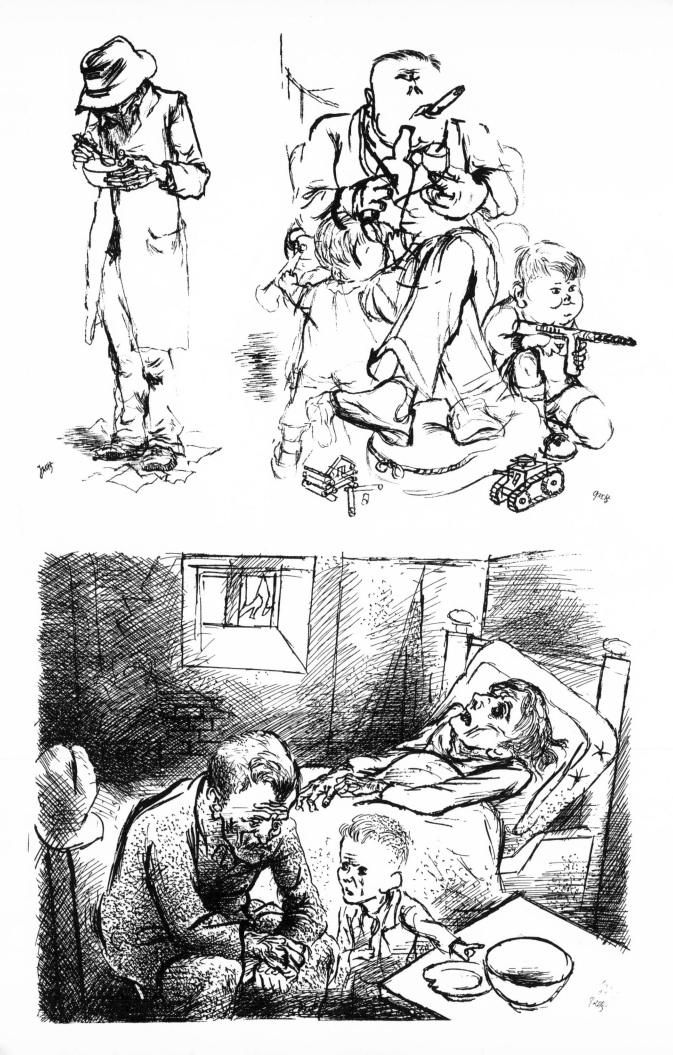

62

63

The ambassador of good will

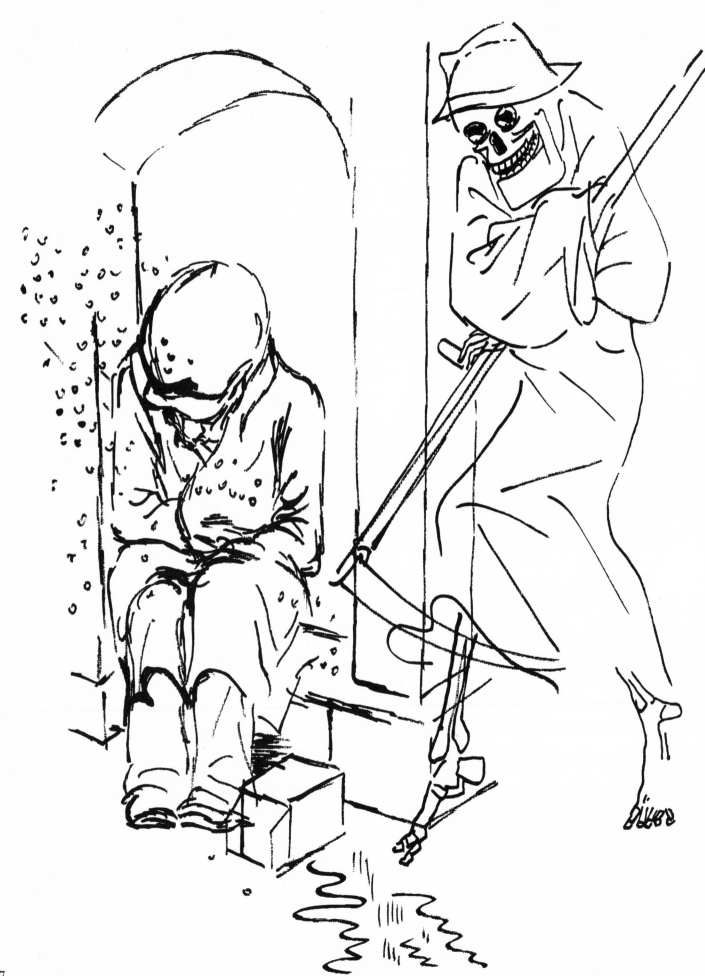

69

Bauernwagen

71

72

74

75

76

7

78

79

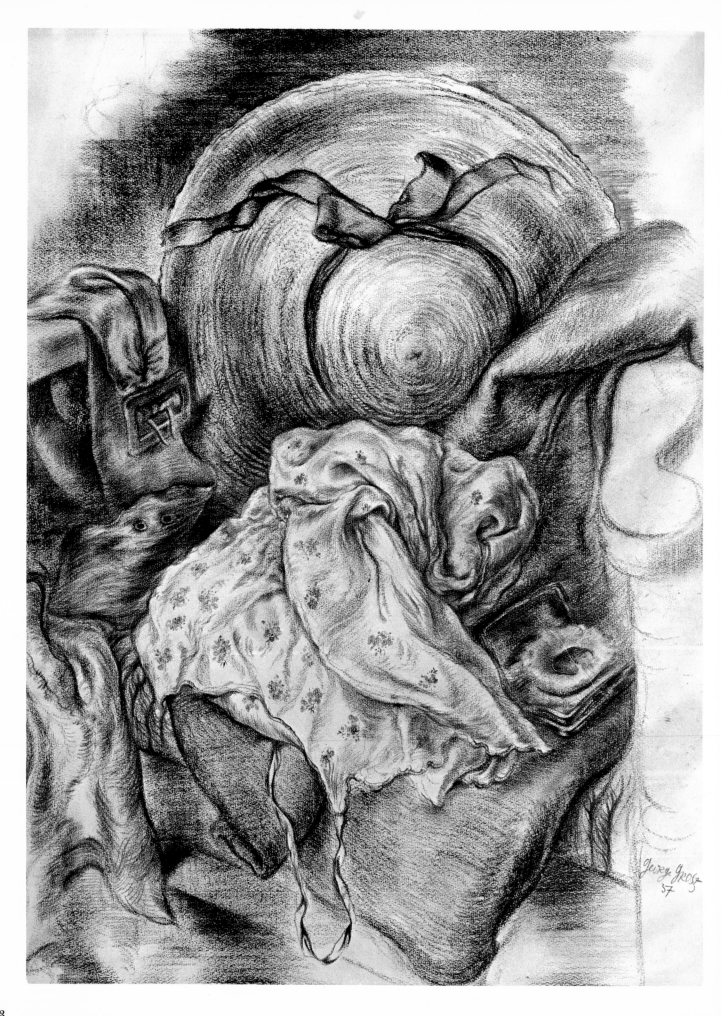

84

85

89

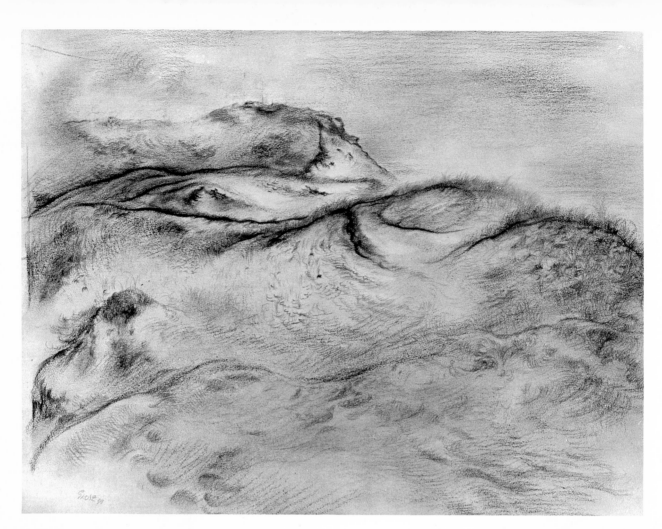

91

92

George Grosz
...Archiving
April 1945
Douglaston

96

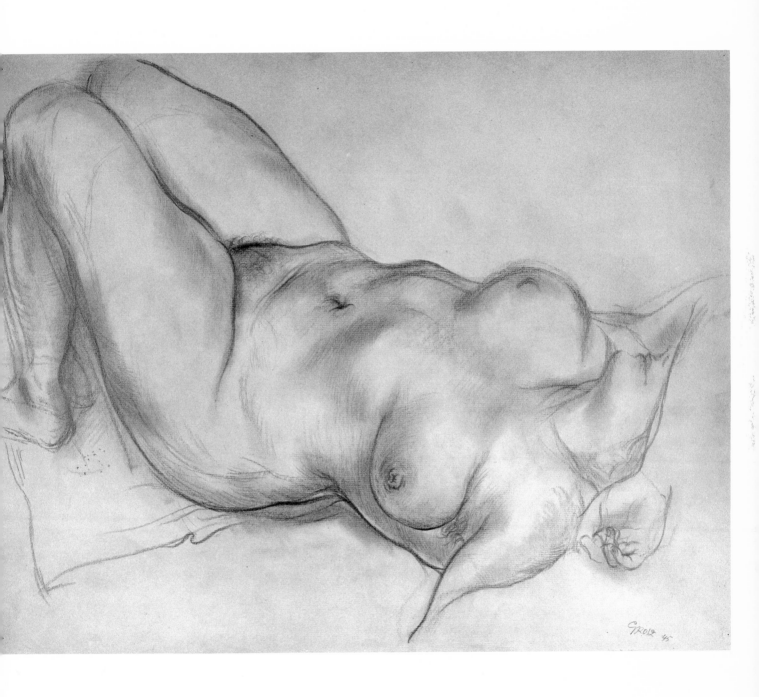

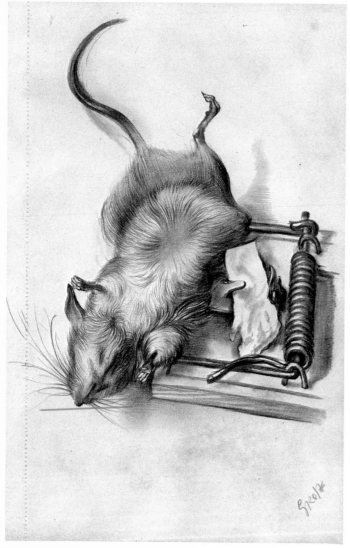

102

103

104

105

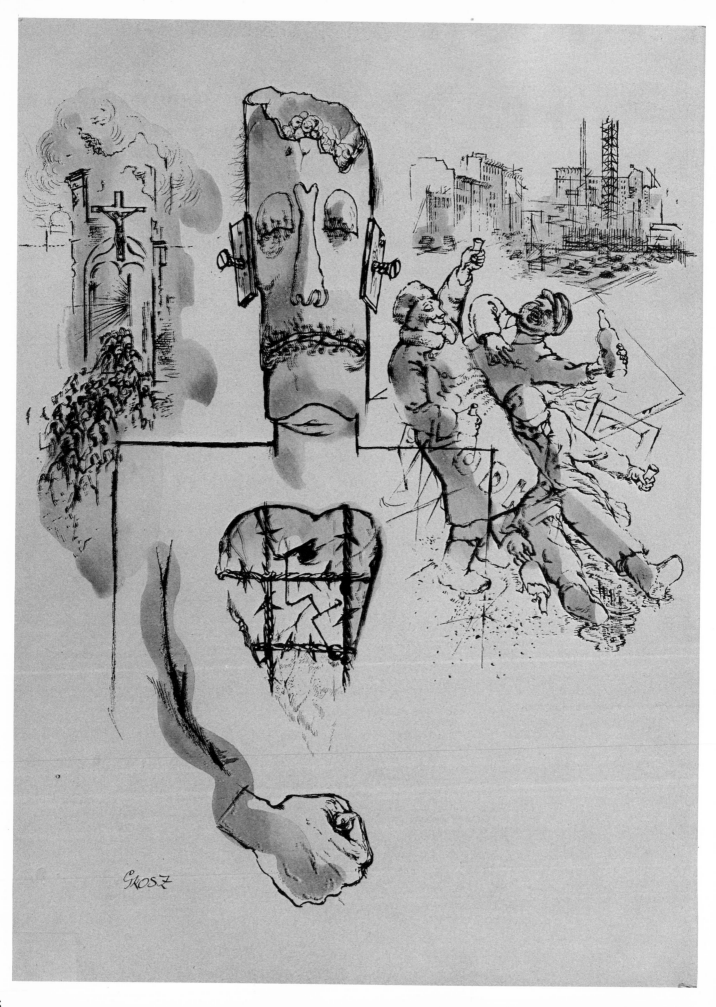

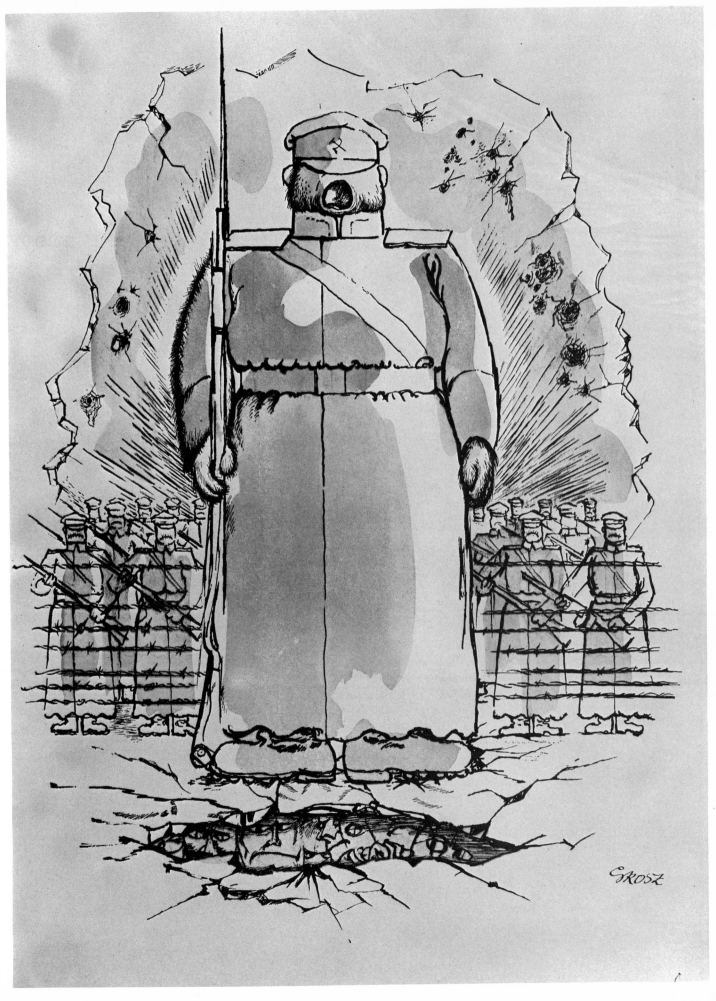